Moral Reasoning

An Intentional Approach to Distinguishing Right from Wrong

Michael S. Jones

publishing company

Cover image © Shutterstock, Inc.

Kendall Hunt
publishing company

www.kendallhunt.com
Send all inquiries to:
4050 Westmark Drive
Dubuque, IA 52004-1840

Copyright © 2017 by Michael S. Jones

ISBN 978-1-5249-4530-5

Published in the United States of America

Contents

Dedication: To my colleagues Dr. Mark Foreman and Dr. David Baggett, who have been a constant source of advice and encouragement as I teach ethics at Liberty University, and to God, the ultimate source of moral wisdom. James 3:17, "But the wisdom that is from above is first pure, then peaceable, gentle, and easy to be intreated, full of mercy and good fruits, without partiality, and without hypocrisy."

Preface

As I approached the task of writing this volume, I realized that one might well ask, "Why another ethics textbook?" There are many short introductions to ethics on the market already. This introduction is specifically Christian, which sets it apart from many of the others, but it's certainly not the only Christian introduction to ethics. My justification for this project is that in my own teaching I find a need for a specific sort of introduction that is not currently available elsewhere: an elementary introduction to Christian ethics that focuses on the theoretical side rather than the practical. This book is intended to combine three attributes in a complementary fashion: 1. It is very approachable, but 2. At the same time it focuses on theoretical issues rather than applied ethics, and 3. It explicates an approach to ethics that I believe to be both consistently Christian and philosophically satisfying.

This book makes little attempt to apply metaethical theories to real-life dilemmas. For an approach that balances theory with application, it would be best to utilize this book in conjunction with another that focuses on applied ethics. Good examples of such books are:

- David K. Clark and Robert V. Rakestraw, eds., *Readings in Christian Ethics: Issues and applications* (Grand Rapids, MI: Baker Academic, 1995).
- Anne and Owen Smith, *Taking Sides: Clashing views on moral issues*, 14th ed. (New York: McGraw-Hill, 2014).
- Laura A. Stivers, Christine E. Gudorf, and James B. Martin-Schramm, *Christian Ethics: A case method approach* (Maryknoll, NY: Orbis Books, 2012).

Naturally an introductory book like the present volume does not attempt to cover every possible approach to ethics. This is why, in spite of my own interest in comparative philosophy, I do not introduce non-Western ethical traditions like Buddhism and Confucianism and contemporary Western perspectives like feminist ethics and Postmodernism. Those interested in reading about these traditions can find them described and discussed in many longer ethics textbooks.

My goal in this volume is to provide a very approachable guide for Christians to Western philosophical ethics. I am a Christian and I have found much in the Western ethical tradition that has helped me to form a more systematic and comprehensive approach to Christian ethics. Now I want to help others make the same sorts of discoveries. Some readers may be wondering why a Christian would concern himself (or herself) with philosophical approaches to ethics when we can simply look to the Bible to determine what is morally right and morally wrong. This is an important question to which I will return at the appropriate time. For now, I will simply say that studying philosophical ethics can actually help us to better understand the ethical insights that are implicit in the Bible, and hence studying philosophical ethics can help us to better understand Christian ethics.

Because this volume is intended to be used as a textbook, it contains a number of features designed to make it more effective to beginning students of ethics. Each chapter begins with a synopsis that very briefly explains what the chapter is about. Each chapter is followed by a series of questions for the reader to think about. Following these questions is a list of key terms, and where that vocabulary is explained in the chapter the term is printed in bold. Each chapter is also followed by a list of suggested further readings. The book focuses on ethical theories rather than important historical figures, but sidebars are used to introduce the most significant thinkers associated with each ethical theory discussed. Finally, the book ends with an extensive index. I believe that these features will enhance the reader's learning experience.

Chapter One

"Intentional" Ethics

Synopsis

This chapter explains why the study of ethics is important and what the main goals of this book are. It also introduces the distinction between ethics and morality and the distinction between "metaethics" and "applied ethics."

Introduction

Everyone encounters moral dilemmas. Sometimes they are big and obvious, like the temptation to cheat on your homework or your taxes. Sometimes they are much smaller, like when you are tempted to slightly exceed the speed limit in order to make it to work on time,[1] or much more opaque, like when you must choose between options that seem equally bad or that have a complicated mixture of desirable and undesirable consequences.

Clearly morality is something that affects every one of us. And we all have opinions on moral issues – often very strong ones! But while most people seem to be aware of what their opinions are, most do not seem to be able to explain where their opinions come from or how they know that their opinions are true. In other words, few people can adequately justify their moral beliefs.

The goal of this book is to enable you to be among those who can in fact explain where their moral convictions come from and how they are justified in believing them. Being able to do this is important, for it enables you to

---

[1] Some would argue that breaking the speed limit is a legal issue rather than a moral one. The distinction between what is moral and what is legal is an important one, but one that is beyond of the scope of this book. In using the example of breaking the speed limit I am assuming the position that people are morally obligated to comply with the law unless doing so would result in a greater immorality than not doing so, but I will not attempt to defend that position here.

know that your convictions are not merely unfounded opinion. Furthermore, it prepares you to approach future moral dilemmas in a way that will maximize the likelihood that you will arrive at the best conclusions. That is what "philosophical ethics" is all about.[2]

Theory

The term **ethics** refers to a theory about what is morally right and wrong. It is similar to the term **morals** except that the latter sometimes refers to a person's pre-theoretical beliefs about what is right and wrong while the former refers to beliefs about right and wrong that have been carefully thought about and thus are reasoned, intentional conclusions on the matter.

    This brings us to the subtitle of this book: "An intentional approach to distinguishing right from wrong." In this context I am using the term "intentional" to mean "deliberately and carefully thought through." Many people simply absorb their moral beliefs from the culture in which they are raised. However, different cultures sometimes contain very different systems of moral belief. For example, the moral beliefs of a Wahhabi Muslim culture contrast sharply with the moral beliefs of a liberal western European culture. Sometimes these belief systems are not merely different: sometimes they are incompatible. In a situation where one set of beliefs contradicts the other, the principle of non-contradiction (one of the most fundamental principles of logical though) indicates that

---

[2] "Philosophical ethics" is the approach to ethics that tries to understand and evaluate issues relating to morality via careful, rational thought. It can be contrasted with other approaches to ethics, such as "biblical ethics," which tries to evaluate moral issues in light of the teaching of the Bible, and "descriptive ethics," which limits itself to describing ethical systems without evaluating them.

they cannot both be true. It would verge on arrogance to simply assume that my culture got it right and another culture got it wrong. Such a position should only be adopted after a careful, objective analysis of the competing systems. Therefore it is not a good idea to simply adopt the morality advocated by my culture lest I be guilty of arrogance – and lest I inadvertently adopt a morality that is mistaken.

My goal for you, the reader, is to get you to evaluate the options and then intentionally choose a system of moral beliefs. At this moment it is quite possible that you have moral beliefs that you have never thought through carefully. These beliefs could be mistaken and you wouldn't even know it. By the time you are finished reading this book you will be able to evaluate your moral beliefs – and why you believe them – and determine for yourself whether or not they are true.

I've mentioned (and briefly defined) the terms "ethics and "morality." Let me briefly comment on a third, related term: "**etiquette**." Etiquette has to do with the behavioral expectations of a given society. When you do what is expected of you, then you have good etiquette. If you do not do what society expects, then you have committed a *faux pas* (which is the French term for a "miss step" – a slip up). Wearing casual clothes to a formal occasion is poor etiquette. People will likely look askance at you as if you have done something wrong. And you have, in a sense. But you haven't done anything immoral – it's not wrong in the specifically moral sense. Potentially there is a huge difference between what your culture expects of you and what is morally right. This is a point to which we'll return in the next chapter. For now, I'll simply share with you a quote from the late 20th century philosopher Louis Pojman: "Etiquette is a cultural

4

invention, but morality claims to be a *discovery*." (Thought provoking, isn't it?)[3]

Broadly speaking, the study of ethics can be divided into two major areas: metaethics and applied ethics.[4] The prefix "meta-" indicates something lying beyond or behind something else, such as in the term "metalanguage" (which is a language created to talk about language) and "**metaphysics**" (which is the attempt to get beyond our assumptions about reality in order to investigate its true nature). In the case of **metaethics** we are talking about the attempt to see "behind the scene" of someone's moral presuppositions in order to discover and evaluate the beliefs and methods on which they are based. For example, if someone believes that abortion is immoral, that belief is almost certainly based on several other beliefs, perhaps including the belief that a zygote/embryo/fetus is a developing person and the belief that ending its life is morally equivalent to ending the life of an infant or child. This could be coupled with a theory about why it is immoral to kill children, etc. Metaethics examines such presuppositions and theories in an attempt to evaluate them in order to determine whether or not the belief that they support is justified.

Applied ethics is what most people think of when they hear the terms "ethics" and "morals." It is the attempt to evaluate the morality of specific actions such as abortion, infanticide, euthanasia, capital punishment, and many, many others. (These examples happen to involve ending a life, but applied ethics addresses many other sorts of actions, too, in a wide range of fields including art, finance, government, medicine, religion, sports, and on and on.)

---

[3] Louis Pojman, ed. *Moral Philosophy: A Reader*, 4th ed. (Indianapolis, IN: Hackett, 2009) xi.
[4] Many ethicists differentiate between metaethics and normative ethics, while others consider normative ethics to be a subset of metaethics. In this book I am going to follow the latter example.

METAETHICS:

- Is morality culturally relative?
- Are there moral absolutes?
- What is the basis of morality?
- How can we know what is right and wrong?
- Which method of distinguishing right from wrong is most effective?
- etc.

APPLIED ETHICS:

- abortion
- capital punishment
- drug usage in sports
- physician-assisted suicide
- slavery
- tattoos
- war
- etc.

In this volume I am going to focus on metaethics, and I believe that there are good reasons for such a focus. As noted earlier, everyone has a set of moral values, but it seems that relatively few people are able to give a coherent and cogent explanation and justification for what they believe. This is in part due to the fact that very few people have ever attempted to systematically evaluate their moral beliefs. In other words, few people have done metaethics. You, the reader, may be just such a person: you probably have quite a few beliefs about what is morally right and wrong. Do you support or oppose abortion? Do you have an opinion about capital punishment? Do you think it's wrong to smoke cigarettes or marijuana? Do you think it's morally right to help people in need – perhaps volunteering at a soup kitchen, or supporting a child in an impoverished society through World Vision or Compassion International? We all have such beliefs. But how strong of a defense can you give for these beliefs? How do you know that your opinion that smoking marijuana is wrong is actually true? There are many who believe that use of medical marijuana is moral and some who believe that recreational use of marijuana is moral, too. You can't simply dismiss these people as irrational: some of them may be, but not all of them are. If you doubt this, take a look at Douglas Husak's article, "Liberal Neutrality, Autonomy, and Drug Prohibitions."[5] This is a sophisticated and very intelligent argument for legalizing recreational use of drugs.

There are several advantages to focusing on metaethics in this book. Having a solid grasp of metaethics allows us to: 1. Critically evaluate our own moral convictions. 2. Critically evaluate other people's moral convictions 3. Effectively advocate on behalf of what we think is morally right. 4. Thoughtfully and intentionally

---

[5] Douglas N. Husak, "Liberal Neutrality, Autonomy, and Drug Prohibitions," *Philosophy & Public Affairs* 29:1 (January 2000): 43-80.

construct an ethical system of our own choosing rather than simply adopting whatever ethical beliefs are most prevalent in our culture.

At this point I'd like to anticipate some possible objections to what I've been arguing – that each of us needs to study metaethics in order to be able to critically evaluate our moral presuppositions and intentionally construct a coherent and cogent ethical system. Some people might respond to this with an appeal to "common sense." In fact, many people think that moral knowledge comes to us via common sense and that those who do not have clear moral vision are either devoid of common sense or are ignoring what their common sense is telling them. Those who hold to this view often react negatively to the suggestion that people need to or ought to carefully think through their moral beliefs in order to know if and how they are justified. They are convinced that what is morally right is obvious to anyone who sincerely cares to know.

I think there is some truth to this, but less than some people suppose. We must begin by asking ourselves what common sense is and where it comes from. Some seem to think that common sense is a sort of innate knowledge built into the minds (or hearts) of the human race, perhaps something put there by God, and that as such common sense is an unfailing guide to truth. As a Christian ethicist, I am sympathetic to this view of the origin of common sense, for in the second chapter of the biblical book of Romans the apostle Paul mentions an innate moral sense possessed even by those who do not have access to the Hebrew Bible (the Old Testament).[6]

---

[6] Romans 2:14-15: "For when the Gentiles, which have not the law, do by nature the things contained in the law, these, having not the law, are a law unto themselves: which shew the work of the law written in their hearts, their conscience also bearing witness, and their thoughts the mean while accusing or else excusing one another...."

More broadly speaking, however, it is easy to see that what is considered to be common sense to people living in one part of the world can vary significantly from what is considered to be common sense in other parts of the world. Even in the United States people have sharp disagreements on what common sense teaches. For example, both Democrats and Republicans seem to think that common sense is clearly on their side. The reason that there are disagreements about the prescriptions of commons sense is that what we think is common sense is heavily influenced by our culture.[7] One person's culture leads him to think that decreasing the number of guns at large in society will contribute to decreasing the amount of gun-related violence in that society, and hence he considers some form of gun control to be common sense. Another person's culture leads him to think that having more armed citizens will render society less vulnerable to malicious gun-wielding assailants and thus he considers gun control to be in obvious conflict with common sense. They both think that common sense is on their side, but it can't be on both sides at the same time, can it? If it can, then what good is it?

So even if there is such a thing as common sense, we need to be able to think critically about what common sense teaches and even about whether we should always be in agreement with it. For it seems that common sense can be mistaken – it was mistaken about the divine right of kings throughout much of European history and about the

---

[7] I am inclined to think that common sense is largely a product of culture and history rather than some sort of divinely-implanted knowledge. This does not, however, mean that it is of no value, for it is based on what people have experienced over and over again. These experiences lead to certain beliefs that are justified by those experiences and often reflect solid conclusions, principles, or practices. However, like any human belief, the deliverances of common sense can be mistaken.

equal rights of African-Americans in the antebellum South, and it can be mistaken today. So even if there is common sense, we still need metaethics.

Another possible objection to studying metaethics is that it is not needed by Christians since we can simply look in the Bible to find answers to all of life's moral dilemmas. Again I am not completely unsympathetic to this, for I consider the Bible to be an invaluable resource for ethics. However, I cannot completely agree with this sentiment, either. The reason for this is that those who have studied metaethics will be in a much better position to discover and understand the ethical insights of the Bible than are those readers of the Bible who have not studied metaethics. I see this every time I teach ethics and discuss the moral implications of various biblical passages: my students are sometimes completely oblivious to the moral reasoning that lies just beneath the surface of the passages that we discuss. I am convinced that the most fruitful approach to ethics combines a philosophical study of metaethical theories and a hermeneutically-informed reading of the Bible. The idea that the Christian ethicist must choose between careful philosophical reflection and careful reading of the Bible clearly involves a **false dilemma**.[8]

A third objection is more epistemological in nature.[9] There are people who object to any moral standard by exclaiming, in effect, "That's just your opinion." This seems to be a form of skepticism aimed specifically at

---

[8] A "false dilemma" is a logical fallacy that involves either artificially limiting someone's choices to fewer options than are really possible (like saying that a person must be either pro-life or pro-woman, when in fact many who are pro-life are emphatically pro-woman as well) or, as here, forcing someone to choose one or the other of two options when in fact the person could take both (would you like breakfast or lunch today?). The best Christian ethic will involve careful thinking as well as careful Bible-reading, not one or the other.

[9] **Epistemology**, very briefly defined, is the study of how we know what we know.

ethics. The underlying belief may be that moral values are nothing more than opinions, or perhaps it is that even if such values are more than mere opinion, there is no way to know which opinion is actually the correct one. Regarding the latter, there are actually quite a few possible ways of evaluating competing moral opinions to determine which is more likely to be correct, and these are what the bulk of this book will cover. The former view is a version of ethical relativism, which is such a significant threat to developing a coherent ethical system that it will be the subject of a whole chapter – the very next chapter. So please read on!

Questions to Ponder:

- What is the difference between "ethics" and "morals"?
- Where did you get your own ideas about what actions are ethical and what actions are not?
- What does it mean to be "intentional" about something?
- What is "common sense" and what role should it play in ethics?
- How important is "metaethics"?
- What role should the Bible play in the study of ethics?

Terms to know:

- Ethics
- Morality
- Etiquette
- Metaphysics
- Metaethics

- Applied ethics
- Epistemology
- False dilemma

For further reading:

Some introductory books on philosophical ethics that are written from a Christian perspective are the following:

- John S Feinberg and Paul D. Feinberg, *Ethics for a Brave New World*, 2nd ed. Wheaton, IL: Crossway, 2010.
- Dennis P Hollinger, *Choosing the Good: Christian Ethics in a Complex World*. Grand Rapids, MI: Baker Academic, 2002.
- Arthur F. Holmes, *Ethics: Approaching Moral Decisions*, 2nd ed. Downers Grove, IL: InterVarsity Press, 2007.

More general resources on philosophical ethics:

- Lawrence C. Becker and Charlotte B. Becker, eds., *Encyclopedia of Ethics*, 2nd ed. New York: Routledge, 2003.
- Vernon Bourke, *History of Ethics, vols. 1 & 2.* Edinburg, VA: Axios Press, 2007.

Chapter Two

Ethical Relativism

Synopsis

In this chapter we define and discuss various forms of ethical relativism. We consider reasons for thinking that relativism is true and reasons for thinking that it is false. In the end it seems that the arguments against relativism are much stronger than the arguments in its favor.

Introduction

Have you ever had anyone tell you, "Well, that may be right for you, but it's not right for me"? It could be that the view underlying this statement is **ethical relativism**. Ethical relativisms come in various forms, but the common thread that binds them together is the idea that what is actually right and wrong can vary from one person or group of people to another. While this has never been the dominant view in the West, it gained ground throughout the 20th century and with the entrance of Postmodernism into public consciousness it has become a major factor in Western culture.

If ethical relativism is true, then the approach that we must take to determining what is morally right will be very different from the approach that we would take if relativism is not true. Hence it is very important to treat this issue near the beginning of a book on metaethics.

One type of relativism is essentially epistemological in nature. It argues that moral judgements are completely subjective; that is, it holds that there is no possible way to be objective about morality. This view is called "**moral subjectivism**."[10] It may at first seem strange to the reader

---

[10] The opposite of moral subjectivism is **ethical objectivism**, which holds that ethical principles are not completely subjective but rather can be known objectively.

who has never encountered it, but it's not so odd: after all, we have no problem saying that what kind of food tastes best, what kind of music sounds best, and what kind of painting looks best are completely subjective issues. "Beauty is in the eye of the beholder," as they say. Essentially the moral subjectivist is saying that morality is also a matter of personal taste or preference. One person prefers a society in which taxes are high in order to provide social benefits for even the neediest people in that society, while another person prefers a society in which both taxes and social benefits are minimal in the belief that this will result in a thrifty and industrious working class. Obviously there are advantages and disadvantages to both of these approaches; perhaps which is best is simply a matter of taste. That is what the subjectivist would argue, anyway.

Another type of relativism is "**cultural relativism**." This is the view that what is right or wrong is determined by your culture, by the society in which you live. The culture of the United States values independence, self-reliance, resourcefulness, and the Protestant work ethic (among other things). A cultural relativist would say that what is right in our context is what is in accord with these values. Therefore a socio-economic approach that tends to be in opposition to high taxes and broad social benefits is the more ethical option in the US. In contrast, Chinese culture (even prior to the ascent of Chinese communism) values the whole above the parts, seeing humanity as an ascending hierarchy the preservation and flourishing of which is the greatest good. Hence the family unit is of more importance than the individuals who make up the family, the village is of more importance than the families that make up the village, and the state is of more importance than the villages that make up the state. But that which benefits the state tends to benefit the village, and that which benefits the village tends to benefit the family, and that which benefits the family tends to benefit the individual.

And acting in a self-sacrificial way in order to benefit the next superior unit can actually be what is in the best interest of the unit that is sacrificing. This, according to the cultural relativist, explains why a socio-economic approach that supports high taxes and broad social benefits is the more ethical option in China.

Many, many examples of cultural relativism can be given. In some indigenous cultures women wear no shirts and this causes no scandal. It doesn't cause men to lust after them; in fact, men don't even notice. However, if a woman walks across the campus of a university in North America with her upper body unclothed, that would probably be more than merely a *faux pas*. It would be immoral, for it would both contradict the **mores**[11] of American culture and potentially cause lustful thoughts in the minds of some who see her. But in the USA it is common for women to wear short skirts, halter tops, and to swim in public wearing swim suits that cover very little of their bodies. This is accepted in the American culture, but can you imagine what would happen if a woman were to dress that way in public in Saudi Arabia? What Americans take to be moral is not the same as what people in other parts of the world take to be moral. And here's the kicker: each moral system – be it in an indigenous culture, in North America, in China, or in Saudi Arabia – works for the people living therein. According to cultural relativism, each society or culture has its own system of moral values that in effect determines what is morally right and wrong in that society.

---

[11] In ethics the word "more" is pronounced "moray," just as in moray eel. Mores are moral values shared by a group of people.

Ruth Benedict

Ruth Benedict was a very influential 20th century American educator, anthropologist, author, and poet. She authored books on cultural anthropology, American Indian culture, Japanese culture, and racism. She taught at Colombia University, served as the editor of the *Journal of American Folklore*, and was the president of the American Anthropological Association. Her work in cultural anthropology lead her to view many things through the lens of culture, including ethics. Since so many other parts of human life are a byproduct of culture, it's not surprising that she would conclude that morays are as well.

Cultural relativism is more metaphysical than is moral subjectivism, which is more epistemological in nature. That means that cultural relativism is not merely talking about what we perceive as being right and wrong (remember that epistemology has to do with how we know things) but rather what actually *is* right and wrong (metaphysics has to do with the actual nature of things, not simply our perceptions of them). According to cultural relativism, each culture or society actually determines what is right or wrong for those living in that culture or society. If your culture says that something is wrong, then, according to this view, it is immoral for you to do it.

Arguments for Relativism

Why would someone think that morality is relative? Well, we've already seen some examples of the sort of evidence that leads some people to this conclusion. Some take the wide diversity of ethical systems and moral convictions found throughout the world as evidence that there are no universal moral truths. This has been called the argument from the "diversity thesis." The **diversity thesis** affirms that there are no moral principles that are held by all people (there are no "**universals**"). Based on this evidence, relativists draw two conclusions: 1. Moral values are cultural constructs, and 2. There are no moral absolutes. (A **moral absolute** is an ethical principle that is binding on all people rather than just the people in a specific culture or society.)

Whether relativists are correct that there are no universal moral truths is open to debate,[12] but they are

---

[12] There are a number of moral values and principles that have been defended as being universal. One example is the Golden Rule ("Do

obviously right that there is a great deal of diversity on moral issues. However, even if the denial of moral universals can be sustained, many ethicists are concerned that the argument from the diversity thesis to relativism is a **non sequitur**.[13]

It seems that the problem here is an unfortunate **conflation**[14] of the concepts of "universal" and "absolute." The former refers, as previously stated, to a moral value that is acknowledged by all people – a value that occurs universally throughout the human race. There may not be any universals, but that doesn't necessarily show that there are no absolutes – no ethical principles or values that *should* occur universally throughout the human race.

For example, a moral value held by at least some societies is that it is wrong to torture innocent people. This may not be a universal, for there may be some who think that it is acceptable to torture innocent people. But perhaps those who think torture is OK are simply mistaken, and perhaps it really is wrong to torture innocent people. If that is the case, then even though "thou shall not torture innocent people" is not a universal (for it is not universally accepted) it is still an absolute. Universals and absolutes are not the same thing, and proving that the former do not exist does not prove the nonexistence of the latter.

This, of course, does not prove that there actually are absolutes. It simply shows that disproving the existence of universals – if that can be done – does not also disprove

---

unto others as you would have them do to you"), which appears in religions and philosophies from every part of the world in very diverse epochs. See Leonard Swidler, "Toward a Universal Declaration of a Global Ethic," *Journal for the Study of Religions and Ideologies* 3, no. 7 (Spring 2004): 33-6 http://jsri.ro/ojs/index.php/jsri/issue/view/9 (accessed 11 February 2016).

[13] A "non sequitur" is a fallacy committed when the conclusion doesn't follow from the premises that are used to support it.

[14] Conflation is the combination of two distinct ideas as if there are no relevant differences between them.

the existence of absolutes. Those who maintain that relativism is mistaken should go on to give reasons for believing that there really are ethical absolutes. Can that be done? Well, at the very least it can be stated that there are some actions that are very difficult to conceive as not being absolutes. For example, could it ever be immoral to "love God with all your heart and love your neighbor as yourself," as Jesus put it? If not, then this principle (or these two principles, if you prefer) would be a positive ethical absolute. Can you imagine a time when it would ever be right to torture a child simply for the fun of it? If not, then this seems like a strong candidate for a negative ethical absolute (a moral prohibition).

Now let me return to the first conclusion that the relativist draws from the diversity thesis: moral values are cultural constructs. A "cultural construct" is a belief, value, or tradition that is created by and becomes part of a particular culture. When someone asserts that morals are cultural constructs she is saying that morals don't exist independently of culture but instead are created by a culture, perhaps unconsciously over a long period of time in response to certain events that take place in that culture or certain needs of the people in that culture. For example, a cultural relativist might point out that for most of the known history of the human race owning slaves was not considered immoral, but today slavery is widely considered immoral. She would then argue that contemporary culture has developed a moral value that was absent in earlier cultures: human freedom.

Once again the relativist has hit on some truth. There certainly are things that we consider moral and immoral today that were not considered moral or immoral at other times. In fact, there are quite a few such things, and some of them are very significant – equal rights for women and minorities, for example. But the underlying argument, that the diversity thesis shows that moral values are cultural constructs, seems to commit the very same fallacy that is committed when the relativist uses the diversity thesis to argue that there are no ethical absolutes. Both arguments appear to rely on conflation. In this case what is conflated are the concepts of moral values and ethical absolutes.

In essence the relativist is overlooking the distinction between epistemology and metaphysics. The term "moral values" connotes what people believe is right or wrong: their opinions. The term "ethical absolutes," on the other hand, refers to what actually is right or wrong independent of what people think. If **ethical absolutism** is correct, then binding moral principles do exist (in some fashion – we'll discuss this in a later chapter), regardless of what people believe. You see, the fact that there are a great many opinions about what is right and wrong does not necessarily mean that all (or even several) of the opinions are equally true. (It would be strange if, every time there was widespread disagreement on a subject, the disagreement would be seen as evidence that all of the disputants are equally correct, wouldn't it?) Hence for the diversity thesis to be used as evidence for relativism either the absence of absolutes must be presupposed (which would **beg the question**[15]) or some additional premise or evidence must be added.

One additional piece of evidence that is often thought to be relevant is the observation that those who hold to absolutism seem to have a tendency to be intolerant of those who disagree with them on moral issues. The basic line of reasoning is simple: everyone has a right to his or her own opinion, and therefore people ought to tolerate those who hold to opinions that diverge from their own; absolutism seems to cause people to be intolerant of those whose opinions so diverge; hence absolutism is

---

[15] To "beg the question" is to assume in your proof the truth of the very issue that is being debated. Begging the question is a fallacy, an illogical way of reasoning.

incompatible with the principle that people ought to be tolerant of others opinions. Therefore absolutism should be rejected.[16]

Of course, we all want our opinions to be tolerated by others (or at least most of the time we do – though if we've made a blatant or critical mistake we might not). It would be hypocritical for us to want others to tolerate our opinions but to think that we don't need to tolerate the opinions of others. Hence, at least *prima facie,*[17] tolerance seems to be worth preserving and therefore doctrines like absolutism that undermine tolerance should be viewed with suspicion.

However, with a little reflection a person quickly realizes that the exception mentioned above is actually rather significant, for it encompass a wide range of possible beliefs. For example, very few would argue that we should tolerate the opinions of Nazis wanting to resume the Holocaust or the terrorist belief that attacks on innocent bystanders are a viable way to advance a cause. In fact, the entire legal system seems to be predicated on the assumption that society has the right to limit or even prohibit the practice of many beliefs (the belief that I can drive on public roads at any speed that I want to, that I can take what I want from others without paying, etc.).

---

[16] Formally this can be written as a disjunctive syllogism: either relativism (and tolerance) or intolerance (and absolutism) is to be preferred; intolerance is not to be preferred; therefore relativism is to be preferred. This syllogism is logically valid, but the truthfulness of the premises can be disputed, and therefore the conclusion is also disputable.

[17] *Prima facie* means "at first appearance." A *prima facie* conclusion is a conclusion that one arrives at when one first looks at the evidence on some topic, but such a conclusion may turn out to be wrong, and hence one should not put too much stock in *prima facie* conclusions. A conclusion arrived at after a thorough scrutiny of all the considerations pertinent to the subject being studied is called *ultima facie*.

Now notice that we object to at least some of these beliefs that we do not want to tolerate because of moral values other than tolerance. We object to tolerating antisemitism because antisemitism is a grievous injustice; hence in this context we are valuing justice above tolerance. We object to tolerating terrorism because terrorism is a violation of other people's right to life; hence in this context we value life over tolerance. This suggests that even though we should value tolerance, it is not the only moral value that we prize. We have a range of moral values of which tolerance is one, but it's not the only one. If that is correct, then a careful examination of tolerance results in a defense not of complete relativism but rather of a system of moral values that includes tolerance as one among several (or perhaps many) prized moral values.

This leads to a strong objection to the argument for relativism based on tolerance. If relativism is rigorously true, then there are no ethical absolutes whatsoever. But the preceding discussion brings out the insight that tolerance is itself a moral value. Hence if the relativist is to be consistent, she must reject tolerance right along with all of the other possible ethical absolutes that she is rejecting. However, she cannot appeal to tolerance in defense of relativism and at the same time reject tolerance because it is an ethical absolute and there are no ethical absolutes. If the relativist believes that tolerance is a binding moral value applicable to all people, then in order to avoid contradicting herself she must admit that there is at least one ethical absolute: tolerance. If, on the other hand, tolerance is not such a binding moral value, then an appeal to it as an argument for relativism lacks force.

It seems that the arguments in favor of ethical relativism are not very strong. Logically speaking, that does not mean that relativism can't be true, it only means that relativism hasn't been shown to be true. But there is another way that we could approach the question of the truth or falsity of relativism. We can ask whether it can be shown to be false. Can it?

Arguments against Relativism

There are a number of arguments that attempt to show that ethical relativism is false. One is called "**the problem of specificity.**" Cultural relativism states that moral beliefs are constructed by social groups and hence each set of moral beliefs is binding only within the particular social group that constructed it. But large social groups are composed of smaller social sub-groups, which are themselves composed of even smaller sub-groups, etc. For example, North America is a large social group, one that contrasts sharply with other social groups from around the world. If you've ever attended an international conference with other Americans you may have noticed that even if the Americans are from different parts of the country they usually have much more in common with each other than they do with people from many other parts of the world. However, when you compare the Americans to each other you find that there are also significant regional and class differences. I'm a Pennsylvanian, but I've lived in the Midwest and now I live in the South, and I can tell you about quite a few differences that I've experienced! Even in Pennsylvania there were social sub-groups based on ethnicity, social class, and other things. On the broadest level perhaps all of humanity forms one large social group; on the narrowest level perhaps each individual is his or her own very small social group, having his own cultural peculiarities and moral views.

The question, then, is of which level is the relativist thinking when she affirms that moral beliefs are constructed by and only binding on a social group? Clearly she's not thinking of the whole human race but rather some

24

subset. Is it the nation? Or the region? Or the race? Or the race in that region? Or the class? Or the class in that nation? Or perhaps it's the individual that she should be singling out? It's not clear that there is any good answer to this question. But without a good answer, the view becomes problematically vague, for we no longer have a clear idea what the relevant social group is.

If the relativist takes the broadest view possible (the social group is the whole human race), then even if moral values are social constructs, they are constructs of the whole human race and therefore are binding on everyone. That is as much a version of absolutism as it is relativism, and it's not what relativists are arguing for anyway. If the relativist takes the narrowest view possible (the social group is the individual), then what the cultural relativist is talking about is no different from individual subjectivism, to which we'll return shortly. If the relativist takes any position between these two extremes, then she needs to provide a good reason for taking that position or else her choice is arbitrary. An arbitrary position is not based on a good reason, and therefore there isn't a good reason to think that it is correct.

Regarding individual subjectivism, if it is true, then each person gets to choose not only what to *believe* is right and wrong, but what actually *is* right and wrong. And no one can disagree with what an individual has chosen. So if someone chooses terrorism as his or her morality, then terrorism is right for that person. Whatever a person chooses is right, be it antisemitism, racism, slavery, cannibalism, or whatever else you can imagine. But could that actually be the case? Could antisemitism or racism become moral simply by someone deciding that it's right for her?

The type of argument against individual subjectivism being employed here is called a *reductio ad absurdum*, which is Latin for "reduction to absurdity." A *reductio ad absurdum* works by showing that some principle or idea, if adopted and then followed to its logical end, would lead to a conclusion that is so unlikely that it seems absurd. Here it is being used to show that adopting individual subjectivism would lead to the conclusion that anything at all can be moral if an individual decides that it is moral, which seems absurd. Is torturing children for fun moral just because some sadist decides that it is? Or is it more likely that the sadist is mistaken in his belief that it is moral? I'm strongly inclined toward the latter option, as are most ethicists.

Here's another *reductio* that, like the one above, suggests that there is something amiss with both individual subjectivism and cultural relativism. If relativism is true, then whatever a society (or individual, in the case of subjectivism) currently accepts as being moral actually is moral for that society. If that's the case, then doing anything other than what is currently accepted as being moral is doing something that is not moral. Hence no moral changes should be viewed as moral progress, for they would always involve moving away from what is currently practiced toward something else, which would perforce involve moving away from what is moral toward what is not. In short, if relativism is true, then the concept of moral progress is vacuous.

For example: for much of the history of the world, women have not been viewed as being equal to men. Our history is one of women being dominated by men. If relativism is true, then during those times when male hegemony was accepted as the norm, male hegemony was moral. Hence moving toward a more egalitarian society in which the value and rights of women are on par with those of men would be immoral.

Can that really be the case? Or could it be the case that a cannibalistic society really is just as moral as one that is not cannibalistic, and that a racist society really is just as

Louis Pojman

Louis Pojman was a much respected 20th century American philosopher, educator, and author. He was also an ordained minister of the Reformed Church of America. He held two earned doctorates, taught at many universities in the US and Great Britain, published a very long list of books and articles, and received numerous grants and fellowships. His areas of specialization were ethics and philosophy of religion. While one might expect his ethical thought to flow from his religious convictions and therefore be of little interest to those who are skeptical about religion, in fact he often approached ethics from a common-ground perspective that renders his arguments available to all.

Photo courtesy of Michael S. Jones

moral as one that is not racist, etc.? If you think that these are unlikely, then you should also regard relativism with suspicion.

Conclusion

Relativism begins with some legitimate insights. For one thing, the fact that *moral judgments* are culturally relative seems obvious. This explains the wide diversity of moral views in the world. Furthermore, we can agree that one ought to be tolerant of the views of others as long as those views do not lead to unacceptable consequences. However, neither of these points actually supports the conclusion that there are no moral absolutes once we recognize the important difference between moral judgments and moral absolutes. That the former are relative does not at all entail that the latter are (or that the latter do not exist).

We have seen that the arguments for relativism are not very strong. On the other hand, the arguments against relativism seem pretty convincing. Therefore the most reasonable conclusion is that relativism is mistaken; relativism is not true. If relativism is not true, then objective moral values are not relative. If such values are not relative, then they must be absolute. Hence the conclusion that relativism is not true entails the opposite conclusion about absolutism: absolutism is true; ethical absolutes exist.

If we are right in concluding that absolutism is true, then our metaethical question becomes "What are the moral absolutes?" But in order to answer that question, we must first answer the question "How can we find the moral absolutes?" We turn to that question next.

Questions to Ponder:

- Ask yourself this: If I was a moral relativist, how would I decide what is moral and what is immoral?
- If morality is relative, then what exactly is the difference between a moral act and an immoral one?
- If morality really is relative, then is it ever justified to condemn anyone for any act?
- We've all heard the statement, "Beauty is in the eye of the beholder." How are moral judgements different from judgements about what is beautiful?
- Why are there so many different opinions when it comes to moral issues?
- Are there any moral principles that are accepted by all people everywhere?

Terms to know:

- Ethical relativism
- Moral subjectivism
- Cultural relativism
- Ethical absolutism
- Ethical objectivism
- Mores
- Diversity thesis
- Moral universals
- Moral absolutes
- *Non sequitur*
- Conflation
- Beg the question
- *Prima facie*
- *Ultima facie*
- The problem of specificity
- *Reductio ad absurdum*

For further reading:

- A classic statement of the relativist position (including an implicit move from the diversity thesis to relativism) is Ruth Benedict, "Anthropology and the Abnormal," in *The Journal of General Psychology* 10 (1934): 59-82.
- A longer and more philosophically rigorous argument for relativism is J. L. Mackie, *Ethics: Inventing Right and Wrong*. New York: Penguin, 1990.
- A short but cogent non-religious rebuttal of relativism is provided by Louis Pojman in "A Defense of Ethical Objectivism," in *Moral Philosophy: A Reader*, 4th ed. Indianapolis, IN: Hackett, 2009, 38-59.
- A book-length discussion and critique of relativism is Louis P. Pojman and James Fieser, *Ethics: Discovering Right and Wrong*. Boston: Wadsworth, 2011.

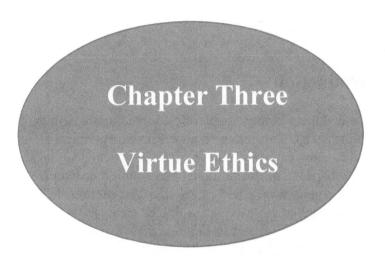

Chapter Three

Virtue Ethics

Synopsis

In this chapter we will begin to examine a range of approaches to discovering the moral absolutes that should guide our lives. These theories are called "ethical theories" or "metaethical theories." First we will look at a simple "list metaethic" and then we will look at virtue ethics. We will evaluate the strengths and weaknesses of both approaches, trying to learn from them while at the same time recognizing their limitations.

Introduction

We ended the previous chapter by concluding that ethical absolutes exist. This led us to pose a new metaethical question: how can we discover what the ethical absolutes are? Perhaps the most traditional and simplest answer to this question is what could be called a "**list metaethic**." This approach to ethics seeks to find or create a list of actions that are moral and a list of actions that are immoral. Then when you are confronted with a moral dilemma all you need to do is consult that list to know which options are moral and which are not.

For example, if you are working on your income taxes and you find that you owe more than you are able to pay, you might have several options, including filing for an extension, borrowing the money that you need to pay your taxes, or reporting less income than you actually received. Since the third of these options is the only one that offers a long-term solution to the problem of having to pay more money than you actually have, you might consider that the best option. However, when you consult your list of right and wrong actions you find that lying is on the list of wrong actions. You know that reporting less income than you actually had would be lying, and so you conclude that reporting less income would be immoral. In this scenario the list metaethic provides concrete guidance on what is right and wrong so that you can think through the options objectively and make the moral decision on how to respond to the dilemma that you face.

Some people think of Christian ethics in terms of a list metaethic. They view the Bible as containing a long list of moral commands and injunctions that should be consulted for guidance whenever we face moral dilemmas. Certainly the Ten Commandments can be viewed along these lines. Of course, the Bible contains much more than simply moral commands and prohibitions. The Medieval Rabbi Maimonides (Moses ben Maimon) counted the commands and prohibitions in the Hebrew Bible and found that there are a total of 613. That's a pretty long list!

However, a list metaethic faces some serious challenges. One is that since the number of possible moral dilemmas that you could encounter during your lifetime is probably much greater than 613, you would need a very long list indeed if you are going to rely on this approach to morality. And how could you know if your list is truly complete? You might think that it contains an answer to every possible dilemma until you run across one that you'd never thought of before, and when that happens, you'd be left without moral guidance.[18]

Another problem is that if you did somehow succeed in compiling an exhaustive list of rights and wrongs, then you'd need to carry that list with you at all times so that when you are confronted by a moral dilemma

---

[18] New moral dilemmas develop over time. For instance, the question of the morality of downloading music or movies from the internet is one that previous generations didn't face. Future generations are likely to face new ethical quandaries that we've never imagined. This shows how any "list metaethic" would face the challenge of always needing to expand its list.

Exodus 20: The Ten Commandments

1. Thou shalt have no other gods before me.
2. Thou shalt not make unto thee any graven image, or any likeness of any thing that is in heaven above, or that is in the earth beneath, or that is in the water under the earth: thou shalt not bow down thyself to them, nor serve them.
3. Thou shalt not take the name of the LORD thy God in vain; for the LORD will not hold him guiltless that taketh his name in vain.
4. Remember the sabbath day, to keep it holy.
5. Honour thy father and thy mother: that thy days may be long upon the land which the LORD thy God giveth thee.
6. Thou shalt not kill.
7. Thou shalt not commit adultery.
8. Thou shalt not steal.
9. Thou shalt not bear false witness against thy neighbour.
10. Thou shalt not covet thy neighbour's house, thou shalt not covet thy neighbour's wife, nor his manservant, nor his maidservant, nor his ox, nor his ass, nor any thing that is thy neighbour's.

Courtesy Library of Congress

you can consult the list for guidance. This would probably require either memorizing the list – which would be quite a challenge for most of us – or perhaps storing it on an electronic device like a smartphone. But if you're relying on carrying it on such a device, you still need to have a thorough understanding of the contents of the list in order to know what to seek when you are confronted by your dilemma. Otherwise how would you be able to find the problem that you are facing on this vast list of ethical commandments that you are carrying around? So there's an indexing problem: how will you find your problem on your list?

Perhaps the most fundamental of all problems for the list metaethic is the problem of how we can know that the entries on our list are accurate. When we are using the Bible as our list, we believe that the list is accurate because it is revealed by an omniscient and truthful God. But we have seen that the biblical list is not exhaustive. Hence we would need to supplement the biblical list in order for it to serve as our list metaethic. But how do we know what to add to the biblical list? How are we going to determine what is morally right and wrong?

This brings us back to our basic metaethical question, and in doing so reveals the fundamental weakness of a list metaethic. A list metaethic does not provide a criterion for determining what belongs on the list, and hence it cannot guide us in constructing the list itself. Therefore this approach fails as a metaethic.

Perhaps a better approach to metaethics would be to seek a principle that can be used in evaluating the morality of actions. A principle would be much easier to remember than a long list of rights and wrongs. Furthermore, a principle could illuminate for us not only what is morally right but also *why* it is right. In other words, it would provide to us the aforementioned criterion of right and wrong.

One such principle was proposed by the famous Greek philosopher Aristotle (384-22 BCE). Aristotle's approach has become known as "**virtue ethics**," and it is experiencing quite a revival among professional ethicists. It deserves to be looked at.

Theory

Aristotle observed that there is a reason for everything that exists. This seemingly simply observation states more than it appears to, though, for here the word "reason" (Greek: *telos* [τελος]) signifies not a *cause* but a *purpose*. And what is true for objects is also true for actions: every action aims at some end, some goal or purpose. When we think about why we do things, we can usually pick out a short-term goal for nearly every act. If we give it more thought, we may even be able to come up with long-range goals toward which our actions move us. What would be the ultimate objective of all of the short-term and long-range goals of your actions? What is it that they are intended – consciously or not – to accomplish? For many people that would be to achieve happiness.

How can a human achieve happiness? Well, lasting happiness – not merely short-term cheerfulness – is a by-product of having a fulfilling life. "Fulfilling" fairly obviously connects with Aristotle's idea of purposefulness (*telos* again): to be fulfilled is a result of satisfying the reason for which you exist. So why do you exist? What is your *raison d'être* (as the French say)?

You've probably heard the expression "a square peg in a round hole." A person who does not know his or her purpose in life can go through life frustrated, as if she is a square peg trying to fit herself into a round hole. It is important to our sense of fulfillment and our lasting

Aristotle

The ancient Greek philosopher Aristotle is one of the most important thinkers of all time. He could be considered the great-grandfather of formal logic and of modern science. His book *Nicomachean Ethics* is one of the earliest attempts at an objective, rational, and fairly systematic approach to ethics in the Western tradition.

"The beauty of the soul shines out when a man bears with composure one heavy mischance after another, not because he does not feel them, but because he is a man of high and heroic temper."

happiness for us to understand what our purpose in life is – what sort of hole we fit into.

Aristotle noticed that the ability to wrestle with moral dilemmas, to make ethical choices, and to have a virtuous moral character are attributes that are fairly unique to the human race. It's debatable whether any other living things share these characteristics. Hence Aristotle concluded that this moral aspect of our being is an indicator of our purpose: we are here to become and to be virtuous people. Through cultivating our inner virtue we become what we are meant to be and through this we find fulfillment in life and the resulting happiness.

This is all well and good, as they say – would anyone who is interested in ethics deny that we should strive to cultivate a virtuous character? But it doesn't really provide us with a criterion for determining what actions are moral (as we were seeking at the end of the previous chapter). So how can we tell what character traits are virtuous? How can we identify true virtues?

A **virtue** is a character trait that inclines you to act and react in a moral way. Aristotle says that virtues strike a balance between two extremes. He calls this the "**Golden Mean**." Examples of this are courage, which strikes a balance between rashness and cowardice, friendliness, which lies between gregariousness and coldness, and patience, which is the happy middle ground between apathy and aggression. So it seems that the criterion that Aristotle is advocating is something like "balance."

As can be seen, the focus of virtue ethics is on cultivating one's inner character. This is a very useful approach to ethics, for when you are faced with a moral dilemma you often need to react immediately. In some of life's most urgent crises you may not have time to meditate on what the right action is. Virtue ethics prepares us for this eventuality by cultivating our inner virtuosity so that when we are called upon to act we respond almost automatically

Plato's Ring of Gyges

One of the virtues that concerned Aristotle was justice. Plato, Aristotle's teacher, told a story about a shepherd who, one day while tending the king's sheep, enters a cave, finds a magic ring, and putting it on, discovers that it makes him invisible. The shepherd uses this newfound power to seduce the queen and usurp the throne. This story occurs in Plato's *Republic* in the context of an argument between Glaucon and Socrates about whether humans are naturally just or only just when others are watching. Glaucon affirms the latter, but Socrates demurs. 2300 years later JRR Tolkien's *The Hobbit* and *The Lord of the Rings* develop this same theme – and it's still a best-seller!

©Skylines/Shutterstock.com

in the way that we should. This approach to ethics requires an intentional cultivation of one's character through practicing right living – as Aristotle pointed out, "For we learn a craft by producing the same product that we must produce when we have learned it; we become builders, for instance, by building, and we become harpists by playing the harp. Similarly, then, we become just by doing just actions, temperate by doing temperate actions, brave by doing brave actions."[19]

According to Aristotle, we can determine what character traits are virtuous by looking for the mean between two extremes. How would he say that we can determine what acts are moral, though? That's simple: we ask ourselves what a virtuous person would do. If a truly virtuous person would not perform some act, then that act must not be moral. If she would perform it, then moral it must be.

Critical Analysis

Virtue ethics has great strength as an approach to preparing yourself for responding to real-life moral dilemmas. It also has the advantage of providing an intrinsic motive for wanting to live virtuously (the prospect of living a fulfilled life). However, it also has several weaknesses.

One weakness of virtue ethics is that it seems to contain at least an element of cultural relativism. The character traits that are valued in one culture may differ widely from those that are valued in another. For example, while humility is a Christian value, in ancient Rome humility was considered to be a vice found only in slaves. Because of this, the evaluation of what constitutes the

---

[19] Aristotle, *Nichomachean Ethics.* Terence Irwin, tr. (Indianapolis, IN: Hackett Publishing Co., 1985), 19.

"Golden Mean" may vary depending on what one's culture teaches about which traits should be valued. The virtue ethicist might respond by arguing that an objective analysis need simply identify the extremes and then find the middle ground that strikes the best balance between them. This seems to presuppose that there is a culturally-neutral perspective from which we can view the options so as to make an objective evaluation. Whether that much objectivity is actually possible is hotly debated.

Virtue ethics also seems to contain a hint of circularity. It argues that we can look to the virtuous person for an example of moral living and that through doing so we can determine what actions are moral. However, if we do not know what actions are moral, it may be impossible to determine who is a virtuous person. This is because a person who is performing immoral actions cannot be virtuous, but we cannot know if a person is thus disqualified from being virtuous unless we already know what actions are immoral. Hence we need to know what is moral in order to determine who is virtuous while at the same time we need to know who is virtuous in order to determine what is moral.

The virtue ethicist might want to argue that we do not need to know what is moral in order to determine who is virtuous: we only need to know what the virtues are. If we grant the distinction between virtuous character traits and moral acts, then the virtue ethicist seems to have a good point. If that's the case, then we are merely left with the difficulty of determining who the virtuous person is in light of the aforementioned element of cultural relativism.

A third problem is perhaps more fundamental: virtue ethics does not provide an explanation of what makes the virtues themselves good. Aristotle seems to think that striking a balance between two extremes is inherently good. However, one could argue that sometimes the extremes are the more pure or more consistent positions and the Golden Mean is the admixture of the two that represents an impure compromise. For example, pure divine holiness is an extreme; some sort of sinful corruption would presumably be the other extreme. What would be the Golden Mean between them? In this case it seems that pure divine holiness is "golden" even though it is not the "mean" between two extremes.

Virtue ethics has much to offer. As we study other ethical theories and begin to formulate our own approach to metaethics, we should keep in mind the lessons that can be learned from Aristotle. But it does not seem that virtue ethics forms a completely satisfactory ethical system all by itself.

Questions to Ponder:

- The Bible contains many moral directives, both commands and prohibitions. How is the biblical approach to ethics different from a "list metaethic"?
- What are the strengths and weaknesses of a list metaethic?
- Does doing good make one a good person or does being a good person result in one doing good? Which comes first?
- What is your telos – your purpose for existing? In other words, why are you here?
- If you had a "ring of Gyges," what would you do with it? Would you live any differently?
- What steps could you take to cultivate your inner virtuosity?

Terms to know:

- List metaethic
- Telos
- Virtue ethics
- Virtue
- Golden Mean
- The Ring of Gyges

For further reading:

- The obvious place to begin reading about virtue ethics is Aristotle's *Nichomachean Ethics*. A good translation is the one by Terence Irwin (Indianapolis, IN: Hackett Publishing Co., 1985). However, *Nichomachean Ethics* is not easy reading.
- A nice introductory volume on virtue ethics is Raymond Devettere, *Introduction to Virtue Ethics: Insights of the Ancient Greeks*. Washington, DC: Georgetown University Press, 2002.
- A more advanced treatment with a contemporary flavor is Alasdair MacIntyre's very influential work *After Virtue: A Study in Moral Theory*. South Bend, IN: University of Notre Dame Press, 1981.
- Another interesting volume on Virtue Ethics is Daniel Harrington and James F. Keenan, *Jesus and Virtue Ethics: Building Bridges between New Testament Studies and Moral Theology*. New York: Sheed & Ward, 2005. Harrington is a New Testament scholar and Keenan is a Roman Catholic ethicist.

Chapter Four

Natural Law Ethics

Synopsis

In this chapter we examine Natural Law Ethics, which is another metaethical theory intended to guide us on our search for moral absolutes. We look at the historical development of Natural Law Ethics, its relationship to Virtue Ethics, and we discuss its strengths and weaknesses.

Introduction

Virtue Ethics is not the only metaethical theory that has its roots in Aristotle. Natural Law Ethics does, too. In fact, Aristotle combined Virtue Ethics and Natural Law Ethics in a complementary way, using each to fill in the gaps of the other.

Theory

In our earlier discussion of Aristotle's ethics we mentioned his view that everything exists for a purpose (*telos*). An implication of this view is that there is a sort of rationality or design behind the universe. Aristotle believed that this design is discoverable through human reason, that by careful investigation we can find out why things are the way they are and what purposes they serve. This belief was a major impetus behind Aristotle's attempts to analyze, classify, and understand the natural world, and it eventually led to the scientific method and the general success of science as we know it today. Science can do what it does because nature has a rational order that the human mind is able to discover.

This Aristotelian background to science is widely recognized by both scientists and philosophers. Less widely recognized are the implications of Aristotelian teleology for ethics. Since ethics is the study of what is morally right and wrong, it is by nature the study of how I ought to interact with the people and objects around me. If everything around me has a purpose, then the ethical way for me to interact with the people and things around me is to act in a way that is informed by and respects that purpose. But I can only do this if that purpose is discoverable to the human mind – which is exactly what Aristotle maintained. Aristotle held that what we in the 21st century call the "laws of nature" are not the only principles governing us and our universe: there are also moral laws woven into the fabric of reality, and a proper ethic reflects these moral laws. Just as in science, these natural moral laws can be discovered through careful rational investigation.

Aristotle does not deny that there are laws, regulations, customs, and the like that are created by humans. He makes a distinction between conventional laws that are *created* by humans and natural laws that are *discovered* by humans. Examples of conventional laws from our day include speed limits, rules of etiquette, and the tax code. This sort of "law" may truly be culturally relative: each society creates its own set of laws, rules, and expectations governing these sorts of things. But Aristotle seems to believe that there is another set of "laws" that are absolute, that are morally binding on all people at all times. He calls these "**natural rights**" (*δικαιον φυσικον*) because they are inherent in nature itself and reflect the purposes (*teloi*) inherent in each thing. These are not created by society or culture but rather are timeless truths that reflect the very nature of reality.

What are the natural laws, and exactly how are they discovered? **Natural Law Ethics** holds that the fundamental principles of ethical conduct are rationally discernible in human nature and the natural world. It holds that through reflecting on the world in which we live,

46

Thomas Aquinas

Thomas Aquinas is an extremely important figure in the history of Western Christianity. He was a great Roman Catholic theologian and philosopher. Born and raised in Italy, he was educated in Italy, Germany, and France. His education included studying theology with very pious monks and philosophy and the sciences with well-travelled and learned university professors. He was convinced that both theology and natural philosophy are valid paths to truth and that the Christian scholar could and should study both. He believed that there is no contradiction between faith and reason.

©Renata Sedmakova/Shutterstock.com

human nature, the basic needs of human flourishing, and the like, we can discern which actions are moral. If, as argued in the previous chapter, part of the human *telos* is to maximize our virtuosity, then actions that enhance that virtuosity are moral; conversely acts that impede the cultivation of our inner virtue are immoral. Some obvious examples come to mind. Acts that rashly endanger one's life are immoral, for if one is not alive, one cannot increase in virtue. Similarly, acts that endanger the lives of others are immoral, for others cannot increase in virtue if they are dead, either. Inasmuch as virtuosity is cultivated through practice (according to Aristotle), and since slavery limits one's freedom to freely practice, slavery is immoral.

These sentiments and this approach to ethics are thought by many to be the (perhaps distant) inspiration behind the opening lines of the *Declaration of Independence* of the United States of America: "We hold these truths to be self-evident, that all men are created equal, that they are endowed by their Creator with certain unalienable Rights, that among these are Life, Liberty and the pursuit of Happiness…" Notice that the author of the *Declaration* thinks that life and liberty are the natural rights of all people – they are not bestowed on citizens by the king or the state. Also notice that he believes that these truths can be discovered by everyone – that's implied by the phrase "self-evident." There does seem to be some strong Aristotelian influence here. However, Aristotle does not connect our natural rights to God as does the author of the *Declaration of Independence*. That was a development in Natural Law Ethics that came later.

Combining Aristotle's ethics with theism began in the early medieval period and was done most prominently by the Muslim philosopher Averroes (also called Ibn Rushd) (1126-98) and the Christian theologian Thomas Aquinas (1225-74). In fact, some current Aristotle scholars think that the way we interpret Aristotle today is largely a reflection of how these two medieval thinkers expounded and expanded Aristotle's ideas.

Those who do not believe in God could, in theory, adopt Aristotle's Natural Law approach to ethics by affirming that the purpose that each thing (and person) has is not bestowed on it by its Creator but rather is simply an aspect of the nature of that thing, a "brute fact" (as they say).[20] They could argue that everything that exists contributes to the world around it in some way and that this contribution is its *telos*. This seems to be a more impoverished sense of "purpose" than what Aristotle actually had in mind, though. He seems to have seen the world in an almost theistic way, as if there is some cosmic intelligence behind everything and that this intelligence bestows meaning and order on the world.[21] Because of this, it is very natural for theistic philosophers like Aquinas to find Aristotle's views easily adaptable to Christianity.

Aquinas sees all that God created as reflecting God's plan for his creation. One aspect of this reflection is the moral aspect, which concerns how humans interact with each other and their environment. For example, treating others as you would want to be treated (the Golden Rule) leads to good relations with those around you; failing to do so can lead to considerable friction (to say the least); so the moral thing to do is to treat others as you would want to be treated. Another example: stewardship of the environment is inherently beneficial to all who live within its confines; rampant consumerism that abuses the environment for short-term gain is detrimental to their long-term wellbeing; therefore an ethic of prudent stewardship is moral while a consumer culture is not.

---

[20] A brute fact is a fact that has and needs no further explanation. This is a controversial idea that we will not discuss further.

[21] An earlier Greek thinker, Anaxagoras, argued explicitly for this, so it would not be a big surprise if Aristotle were to have such an expectation as well.

The Principle of Double Effect

Thomas Aquinas' *Summa Theologica* contains an interesting discussion of the moral status of killing in self-defense. Here he introduces the "Principle of Double Effect," which states that an otherwise good act that has some undesirable consequences (effects) is morally permissible if it meets three criteria:

1. The act itself must be morally good or at least morally neutral.

2. The person acting must intend the good consequences but not the bad.

3. The good consequences must outweigh the bad. (Summa Theologiae, IIa-IIae Q. 64, art. 7)

©corgarashu/Shutterstock.com

Because Aquinas views humans as created in the image of God and thus bearers of an intelligence that reflects God's own (though in a very limited way, of course), Aquinas believes that humans can apprehend God's design and purpose in the created world. Thus he is in fundamental agreement with Aristotle that the moral order woven into the fabric of reality can be discerned by the human mind. However, Aquinas can also appeal to God's special revelation as an additional source for ethics.

A theistic Natural Law ethic fits well with the teleological aspects of virtue ethics: since living virtuously is essentially living in accord with God's design for the created order, living according to God's plan yields a virtuous life. Thus living a virtuous life is quite naturally fulfilling and leads to lasting happiness. Aquinas and other theistic ethicists have not missed this point and typically attempt to combine Natural Law Ethics and Virtue Ethics into a complementary system.

Critical Analysis

Clearly there is much that a Christian ethicist can appreciate in Natural Law Ethics, both in the earlier Aristotelian form and in the later theistic adaptations. However, Natural Law Ethics is not completely beyond criticism. First of all, for those who do not believe that God or anything like God designed the universe, coming up with a cogent explanation of how the universe and the things in it could possibly have a purpose in anything like the Aristotelian sense would probably be very difficult. Some have tried (see the section on suggested readings at the end of this chapter), but Natural Law Ethics seems to fit much more naturally (pun intended) with theism than atheism. Similarly, those who do not believe that there is a discernable rational order in the universe will need to look elsewhere, for Natural Law Ethics is not compatible with this view.

For those who do believe in God and who believe that the universe and the things therein were designed for a purpose, there may still be problems. For Christians like Aquinas there is the problem of depravity. Aquinas holds that humans are created in the image of God and that this involves mirroring God's cognitive capacities at least to the extent necessary to recognize the natural moral law that forms part of the created order. However, this same Christian tradition includes the teaching that humanity has fallen into sin and that this fall has noetic as well as moral consequences. According to most branches of Christianity, our cognitive capacities have been marred by sin to the extent that our ability to recognize and to will the good are both compromised. In the words of the Apostle Paul, "I had not known sin, but by the law: for I had not known lust, except the law had said, Thou shalt not covet."[22] In light of this, the optimism of Natural Law Ethics that unaided human reason is able to reliably discern the fundamental principles of ethical conduct through simple reflection seems problematic.

The Islamic tradition of Averroes does not face the same problem, for Islam does not teach that each human is born with a fallen nature. On this issue Islam is Pelagian.[23] However, there are still challenges for the would-be Muslim proponent of Natural Law Ethics. How are they to account for the widespread disagreement on moral issues if morality is clearly discernable and humans do not have a

---

[22] Romans 7:7. This is a difficult chapter of the Bible but very well worth pondering.

[23] Pelagius was a 4th century Christian theologian who taught that the sin nature is not inherited but rather that each human comes into the world in a sinless state but with the potential to sin, and that other than Jesus of Nazareth, all humans since Adam have failed to maintain this sinlessness while alive on earth.

sin nature? Even devout and learned Muslim scholars disagree on moral issues – sometimes strenuously. If the principles of conduct are evident, then it seems reasonable to expect much more unanimity on ethical issues than there actually is.

Like Virtue Ethics, Natural Law Ethics seems to have some valuable insights but does not seem able to stand on its own as a metaethical theory. Even combined with Virtue Ethics it is not clear that it will succeed. Perhaps here, too, we need to keep in mind the lessons learned but not yet end our search for the most satisfactory ethical system possible.

Questions to Ponder:

- Ask yourself this: If I were a Natural Law ethicist, how would I go about determining if an action is moral or immoral?
- Why would people in the 21st century care about the ethical theories of ancient Greeks like Plato and Aristotle?
- Is morality created or discovered?
- Does every existing thing have a purpose or are some things truly accidental?
- How does Natural Law Ethics complement Virtue Ethics?

Terms to know:

- Natural Law Ethics
- Natural Rights
- Golden Rule
- Principle of Double Effect

For further reading:

- Thomas Aquinas, *Commentary on the Nicomachean Ethics* (translated by C. I. Litzinger. South Bend, IN: Dumb Ox Books, 1993) is a classic discourse on Aristotelian ethics that every ethicist should read. You may need to read it slowly, but it's worth it.
- A good introduction to Aristotle's ethical thought is J. O. Urmson, *Aristotle's Ethics*. Oxford: Basil Blackwell, 1988.
- P. A. Woodward, ed., *The Doctrine of Double Effect: Philosophers Debate a Controversial Moral Principle* (North Bend, IN: University of Notre Dame Press, 2001), is a useful collection of essays on the principle of double effect.
- Philippa Foot, *Natural Goodness* (Oxford: Oxford University Press, 2001), is an attempt to develop a thoroughly naturalistic ethic that builds on the Aristotelian insights of Virtue Ethics and Natural Law Theory.

Chapter Five

Ethical Egoism

Synopsis

In this chapter we examine Ethical Egoism, the theory that says that you ought to do whatever will benefit you the most. We see that this is a consequentialist metaethical theory with ancient roots and a significant contemporary following. We then evaluate strengths and weaknesses of Egoism as an approach to determining what is morally right and wrong.

Introduction

Have you ever been in a position where you simply have to put your own needs or desires before those of others? I remember being with my wife and two children in Romania in a very busy train station. Through circumstances beyond my control, we had arrived only minutes before our train was scheduled to depart. I needed to buy train tickets, but there was a long and very slowly-moving line at the ticket counter. I had no choice but to ask permission to skip to the head of the line. Otherwise we would all be stuck in the city overnight with no place to stay. We felt considerable anxiety about the situation, but happily for me, Romanians are very considerate at times like this and they graciously allowed me to go first, even though they had been waiting in line for a long time. I felt bad about putting my own needs before theirs, but in this case it seemed necessary.

      I felt bad about this because I was raised to not put my own wants and needs before those of others. Hence putting myself first feels unethical to me. There is a theory, though, that says that putting yourself first is the moral thing to do. This view is called "Ethical Egoism" and is the subject of this chapter.

The North Train Station, Bucharest, Romania

Photo courtesy of Michael S. Jones

Theory

On the face of it, a theory that says that you should consistently act in your own self-interest doesn't sound moral. Let's not rush to a hasty conclusion, though. There's more to this theory than you might expect.

Ethical Egoism says that an act can be judged as moral or immoral by looking at its consequences for the person performing the act. If the act is beneficial – if it helps the person to survive, or to thrive, or to be fulfilled, or something along those lines – then the act is moral. If the consequences are detrimental, then the act is immoral.

Because of this emphasis on examining the results of an act, Egoism is considered a consequentialist approach to ethics. A **consequentialist metaethic** is any ethical theory that evaluates the morality of actions by examining their results. This can be done after the fact, looking back at an action and its results and evaluating it based on what the results are known to have been. When consequentialism is used as a guide for action, though, it most often involves attempting to figure out what the future consequences of an action will be and then evaluating the action based upon that expectation.

For example, when I needed train tickets for my family and me, I basically had two options: I could bypass all those who had been waiting in line longer than me, or I could wait in line and miss the train. Doing the former would inconvenience those ahead of me in the line and would show a disregard for their feelings and their situation. It would also require that I do something that makes me feel uneasy – and it would necessitate that I try to quickly and politely explain our need to all of these Romanians in a language that I was still in the process of learning. Those are definitely negatives. However, not doing it would result in my family and me missing the train, spending a long, cold, and uncomfortable night in the train station, and me being late for school the next morning. And while I don't enjoy talking to strangers in a language in which I'm not fluent, doing so won't kill me and might actually help me to improve my mastery of it.

At this point my analysis of the pros and cons of my two options is decidedly consequentialist but not overtly egoistic.[24] This is because the consequences that I have

---

[24] Please note that we are saying "egoistic" rather than "egotistic." An egoist is someone whose choices are based on what is in his or her own

been considering concern many others in addition to myself. I thought about my family, the other people in line, and perhaps even the lady selling the train tickets. An egoist, however, gives priority to the consequences for the individual who is contemplating performing the action. In this train-ticket scenario that is me. In a situation like mine the egoist would ask what the consequences are for me, the one who must make the decision and perform the action. Hence as an egoist I would not concern myself with how the other people in line are going to feel if I cut in front of them. I might, however, give consideration to the feeling of uneasiness that I would feel if I were to butt in line. (It could be argued, though, that I shouldn't feel uneasy if in the end an egoistic analysis shows that butting in line is the right thing to do.) I would not consider the feelings of others or the effects of my actions on others except to the extent that how they feel and how those effects impact me.

Like Virtue Ethics and Natural Law Ethics, Ethical Egoism can be traced all the way back to ancient Greece. Epicurus (341-270BCE) was a Greek philosopher who advocated Egoism. He had interesting reasons for doing so. He believed that everything that exists is composed of atoms. (It's fascinating to think that someone who lived so long before the invention of microscopes would know about atoms, isn't it?) Because of this, Epicurus does not believe in immaterial things like the Christian God or the human soul. Hence he doesn't believe in life after death, heaven, and hell. Therefore for Epicurus morality cannot have anything to do with the will of God, God's commands, or eternal rewards and punishments, as it does in the minds of many religious ethicists. That's why for Epicurus ethics is all about the consequences of our choices for the life that we live on earth.

---

interest. And egotist is someone who thinks that he or she is extra-special and brags about herself all of the time.

Epicurus

Epicurus was an ancient Greek philosopher, a younger contemporary of Aristotle. He was an educator who founded several schools. He also appears to have written prolifically, though many of his writings have been lost. His teaching was very influential, both in his own day and in the following centuries. Some of the Athenian intellectuals who the apostle Paul addressed on his visit to Athens (see Acts. 17) were Epicureans.

Because Epicurus believes that humans are merely physical beings, he sees the greatest value of actions as lying in their ability to benefit our physical and intellectual wellbeing. Hence when Epicurus evaluates an action he asks whether it will make him healthier, happier, safer, more secure, etc. Actions that contribute to the physical and intellectual wellbeing of the one performing the act ought to be done, while those that are detrimental to this sort of wellbeing ought to be avoided.

It must be noted that Epicurus did not advocate an overindulgent, intemperate hedonism. He was too smart for that. Epicurus recognizes that a life of moderation and tranquility is likely to produce, in the long run, greater satisfaction than a life of wild parties that leads to ill health and a troubled psyche. Hence **Epicureanism** emphasizes a balanced life lived in communion with others and focuses on the pleasures of the mind.

Egoism did not die with the ancient Greeks: it is alive and well today. One influential recent proponent is Ayn Rand (1905-82), whose award-winning novel *Atlas Shrugged* (1957) was released as a motion picture trilogy in 2011, 2012, and 2014.

Rand was born in Russia and was a child at the time of the Bolshevik Revolution. Coming from a fairly well-off family, she experienced the injustice and deprivation of the collectivization of property that was imposed by the new Communist government. No doubt this was a formative experience in her life. She eventually was able to emigrate to the United States and became a very outspoken proponent of capitalism.

The heart of Rand's Egoism is the capitalistic view that freeing individuals to seek what is in their own best interest will provide a strong motive for each individual to work industriously to meet her own needs, which in turn will either make her a diligent employee or a resourceful employer. Rand is convinced that each person seeking to better herself results in each person making a greater contribution to society and this unintentionally benefits everyone else. Her ethic is summarized in this short passage from her book *The Virtue of Selfishness*:

> The moral purpose of a man's life is the achievement of his own happiness. This does not mean that he is indifferent to all men, that human life is of no value to him and that he has no reason to help others in an emergency. But it does mean that he does not subordinate his life to the welfare of others, that he does not sacrifice himself to their needs, that the relief of their suffering is not his primary concern, that any help he gives is an exception, not a rule, an act of generosity, not of moral duty.[25]

As a philosopher, Rand did something unusual that contributed greatly to the spread of her ideas: instead of publishing her ideas in dry philosophy textbooks (like this one?), she wove them into the stories of her many novels and plays. In this way her ideas influenced a much larger swath of American (and international) society than they would had she merely published books written for academics. As a result, many of the rank-and-file and also of the leadership of American's more conservative political movements (including libertarians, free-market capitalists, and neo-conservatives) recognize Rand's influence on their ideas.

---

[25] Ayn Rand, "The Ethics of Emergencies," in *The Virtue of Selfishness* (New York: Penguin Books, 1964).

Ayn Rand

Ayn Rand was a prolific, diverse, and creative 20th century author who published essays, short stories, novels, and plays. Many of her works, even her fiction, addressed philosophical issues. Born in Tsarist Russia, she endured Stalinism and had her family's property and business confiscated. She eventually emigrated to the US, where she developed and published her philosophy. She called it "Objectivism." It combines empiricism, critical realism, capitalism, and ethical egoism into a cohesive system. Her most well-known publications are two novels: *The Fountainhead* and *Atlas Shrugged.*

Critical Analysis

Prima facie the thesis that what is right is what is in my own best interest sounds selfish and thus clearly wrong. However, on closer inspection we can see that there are certain positive aspects of giving self-interest its proper due. There are some situations where if you don't look out for yourself no one will. In some communist social systems the welfare of the group has been given so much priority over the welfare of the individual that individuals are deprived of all rights whatsoever (think of Cambodia under the Khmer Rouge).

  In light of Ayn Rand's experiences under communism, her advocacy of Egoism is understandable. However, a philosophy adopted as a reaction to negative life experiences is often an over-reaction, which seems to be the case here. If the protagonists in Rand's novels are her depictions of her vision of the moral person, then her idea of morality involves a degree of sensual indulgence, materialism, and disregard for others that even Epicurus would reject.

  Epicurus' Egoism, on the other hand, seems much less reactionary. His vision of the moral life as one that aims at maximized bodily health and peace of mind seems both more intentional and less self-destructive than Rand's Egoism. Christian readers (and many others) will not agree with Epicurus' atomism and the resulting denial of the existence of immaterial entities like a transcendent God and an immortal human soul. This surely has implications for our approach to ethics. But perhaps there are still Epicurean insights from which we can benefit.

  However, there are other concerns about Ethical Egoism. The first is poses a challenge to any sort of consequentialist metaethic. Consequentialism only works as a means of guiding our actions if we can with some reasonable degree of reliability predict what the consequences of our actions will be. However, it is often very difficult and sometimes impossible to make this sort of prediction. And the more our decision depends on the long-term consequences of the act the more difficult it is to make a prediction with the needed degree of certainty. This is a major concern.

Another aspect of consequentialist metaethical theories to which people object is that they seem to imply that the ends justifies the means. Ethical Egoism seems to say that acts like lying, stealing, and even killing are moral if they bring more benefit to me than harm. I suspect that Epicurus would argue that careful consideration would show that such acts are rarely if ever beneficial to the one performing them, but the impression that I get from Rand's novels is that she would probably disagree with Epicurus on this issue. Who is right? Which is the true egoist? Is it necessarily wrong to say that the ends justify the means? Many ethicists have held that it is.

Another objection arises from the altruistic impulse that most people feel at various times in their lives. **Altruism** is the urge to do something to benefit someone else without any thought or hope of receiving anything in return. If Egoism is correct, then altruistic acts are immoral. But that can't be right, can it? (Note that this is another *reductio ad absurdum*.) The Egoist would probably respond that such acts are not completely selfless, for they give to the one performing them a sense of goodness and self-satisfaction that cannot be achieved in any other way. While this is often the case, by definition this benefit cannot be the chief motive of the act, and thus if there really are altruistic acts, they pose a problem for Ethical Egoism.

Finally, if individuals would only look out for their own best interest as Egoism recommends, what would that do to society? Rand paints the picture of a thriving capitalist society in which people are hard-working, resourceful entrepreneurs. Would that be the outcome, or would it be a cut-throat, dog-eat-dog society, a society of robber barons and chattel, or perhaps one of anarchy? We can hope that the outcome would be Epicurean or Randean, but laissez-faire capitalism has not had such a bright history when it has been tried.

Prima facie the Egoistic position seems to be wrong, and *ultima facie* it fares no better. Despite some significant insights and its considerable influence, Ethical Egoism faces objections that it cannot overcome.

Questions to Ponder:

- Ask yourself this: If I were an ethical egoist, how would I go about determining if an action is moral or immoral?
- How can putting yourself first be ethical? Can it be?
- What role does consideration of consequences play in non-consequentialist ethical theories like Virtue Ethics and Natural Law Ethics?
- Is capitalism inherently egoistic?
- Are truly altruistic acts possible for humans, or do we always act selfishly?

Terms to know:

- Ethical Egoism
- Consequentialist metaethic
- Epicureanism
- Altruism

For further reading:

- Not many of Epicurus' own writings survive, but what does can be found in Bailey Cyril, trans., *Epicurus: The Extant Remains*. Oxford: Clarendon Press, 1926.
- A selection of Rand's writings is Ayn Rand, *The Ayn Rand Reader*, ed. Gary Hull and Leonard Piekoff. New York: Plume, 1999.
- A more contemporary defense of Ethical Egoism is Craig Biddle, *Loving Life: The Morality of Self-interest and the Facts that Support It*. Glen Allen, VA: Glenn Allen Press, 2002.
- A critique of ethical egoism is chapter five, "Ethical Egoism," in James Rachels, *The Elements of Moral Philosophy* 8th edition. New York: McGraw-Hill Education, 2014.

Chapter Six

Utilitarianism

Synopsis

In this chapter we will examine a second consequentialist metaethic: Utilitarianism. We will illustrate its central principle using the universal healthcare debate in American politics. Then we will compare several different approaches to Utilitarianism and discuss its strengths and weaknesses.

Introduction

The previous three chapters have discussed metaethical theories as if they are prescriptions about how we ought to approach moral dilemmas. And that's what they are, in part: they are theories that we can turn to for moral guidance. But this is not all that these theories are: they are also descriptions of various types of people and how they are already viewing morality. The virtue ethicist is convinced that in order to act ethically we need to (and hence ought to) cultivate a virtuous character, the natural law theorist believes that we should seek the guidance provided by our conscience and rational considerations in order to distinguish right from wrong, and the ethical egoist thinks that doing that which would most benefit the one performing the action is morally obligatory. All three of these approaches to ethics can be found in American society. I'm sure that you know people whose default way of thinking about moral issues is dominated by one or the other of these approaches.

It is possible that our fourth metaethical theory is actually the one that is most common in America. The fourth approach is called Utilitarianism, and it seems like a natural fit in a democratic society where we are encouraged from childhood to think about issues in terms of the common good. You yourself may be a Utilitarian – and you may not even know it!

Theory

Utilitarianism says that an act can be judged as moral or immoral by looking at its consequences for everyone affected. The option that produces the most good for the most people (or, when forced to choose between the lesser of two evils, the option that produces the least bad for the least people) is the option that should be chosen. Hence that option is the moral option.

Like Ethical Egoism, Utilitarianism evaluates the morality of an action by examining the results that are likely to follow from it. Thus, like Egoism, Utilitarianism is a consequentialist metaethical theory. But Utilitarianism differs very significantly from Egoism in that the consequences that are considered are not limited to the consequences for the one who is going to perform the act but instead are extended to the consequences for everyone. Before deciding to do something, the Utilitarian asks herself "How will this affect everyone else?" The Utilitarian believes that we should do those things that would result in the most good and least harm for the greatest number of people.

The ongoing debate about healthcare in the USA is a prime example of Utilitarian thinking.[26] Barack Obama, Hillary Clinton, and a great many members of the Democratic Party believe that some sort of universal healthcare orchestrated by the federal government would

---

[26] Similar debates have occurred regarding other large-scale projects of the federal government, such as having a standing army, a national highway system, Social Security, and Medicare. We now take many of these things for granted, but many libertarians argue that they would be better off without the intervention of the federal government.

result in the greatest amount of good for the greatest number of Americans. They see how expensive healthcare is and that there are a great many people who have no health insurance. When faced with an illness, such people have only unattractive options: they can forgo treatment, which can cause them to miss work for prolonged periods of time, or they may be able to borrow money to pay for a doctor's visit, but such loans are often from companies that lend at exorbitant rates, or they can go to the emergency room at a hospital, since emergency rooms are not permitted to turn anyone away. However, the last option has many undesirable results, including overloading hospital emergency rooms with non-emergency patients and passing the cost of such care on to other patients who do have medical insurance or on to taxpayers.

Advocates of universal healthcare point to the large disparity between those who have excellent health insurance and those who have none, the significant burden that uninsured patents place on hospitals all over the country, the large amount of profit that insurance companies are making on healthcare policies, as well as other factors in the current U.S. healthcare system, and argue that a much more equitable healthcare system is possible, one that on a whole provides significantly more healthcare to many more people. A system of universal healthcare would provide medical coverage for everyone, would benefit from economies of scale, could (depending on how it is set up) cut out the costly insurance middle-man, and would completely remove the burden of uninsured patients on hospitals. It might require that some people pay more for coverage than they are currently paying, that some accept less coverage than they currently have, and that insurance companies make considerably less profit from selling health insurance. There definitely would be costs. The argument is that the benefits to the many outweigh the costs, and this is a very Utilitarian argument.

Jeremy Bentham

Jeremy Bentham was an 18th century British philosopher and political activist. Although he is best known for his work on Utilitarian ethics, he also made significant contributions in political philosophy and legal theory. He combined Utilitarian ethics and political theory in a way that foreshadows later legal positivists. Perhaps most importantly, he was the mentor of John Stuart Mill, the most famous of all Utilitarian ethicists.

Those who oppose universal healthcare often respond with equally utilitarian arguments. They argue that universal healthcare would raise taxes for most people, that legislation like the Affordable Healthcare Act (Obamacare) results in health insurance being more expensive for most people, that universal healthcare would result in healthcare itself becoming even more expensive, that if it undermines the healthcare system it could weaken the U.S. economy, etc. All of these arguments are trying to show that universal healthcare would be detrimental to more people than it would help, which is, of course, a Utilitarian argument against universal healthcare. (In addition to Utilitarian arguments, both sides also use other types of arguments in support of their positions.)

As an ethical theory, Utilitarianism feels right to many Americans because we are taught from an early age to have high regard for the welfare of other Americans and to work together for the betterment of our country. However, even if Utilitarianism is correct there are details of the view that need to be discussed and settled. One has to do with the distinction between quantity and quality. What do we mean when we say "the most good"? Are we talking about the greatest quantity without regard for quality, or should we prefer a smaller quantity if it has a very high level of quality? Which would be better, that everyone have an adequate amount of food of a rather ordinary quality, or that some have food at a very high level of quality while others have food that is quite mediocre? That all people have access to education at roughly the same level of quality, or that some have access to very high quality education while others don't? Or to get back to healthcare, that we prefer the status quo or try to work toward a more egalitarian ideal? Which is more important, quantity or quality?

Hedonic Calculus

For Utilitarianism to work, we need to be able to adjudicate between various possible courses of action on the basis of which is going to produce the most good for the greatest number of people. This gives rise to potential problems, though. For example, if I need to choose between an act that will produce a slight benefit to all people effected and one that will provide a major benefit but only to all those who have a significant need, it's not clear which would be the more Utilitarian choice. The first option has the most beneficiaries while the second has the most benefit. Which is the higher priority? Bentham devised a way to determine the right choice: the Hedonic Calculus. By tabulating the certainty, proximity, extent, intensity, duration, fecundity, and purity of an act's benefits Bentham thought that we could objectively adjudicate between it and its rivals.

Jeremy Bentham, a 19th century British intellectual who is in no small measure responsible for the revival of interest in Utilitarianism, thought that the good to be achieved should be understood primarily in terms of quantity. He emphasized this when he said,
"[T]he value which they possess, is exactly in proportion to the pleasure they yield.... Prejudice apart, the game of push-pin is of equal value with the arts and sciences of music and poetry. If the game of push-pin furnish more pleasure, it

is more valuable than either."[27] (Pushpin was a simple children's game of Bentham's day.) For Bentham, trying to decide whether one type of good is higher than another was unnecessary. He may have a good point here, too, for such things are often subjective, a matter of taste, and therefore their quality is not easily compared. (After all, some people really love hamburgers and would prefer a hamburger to a fine lobster dinner; some people would choose banjo music around a campfire over the Royal Concertgebouw Orchestra.) It is simpler to focus on quantity rather than getting tangled in subjective assessments of quality.[28]

Bentham's star pupil, John Stuart Mill, took the opposite position. Mill thought that both quality and quantity are important, and that large amounts of low-quality good do not automatically outweigh smaller quantities of high-quality good. This can be seen to be true in a myriad of examples: not only is it better to have a small quantity of healthy food than a large quantity of junk food, it's better to have one solid house to live in than five dilapidated shanties, it's more enjoyable to hear a story told well than many stories told poorly, in the martial arts one move performed correctly nearly always defeats a flurry of moves performed incorrectly, etc. Mill drives this point home via the following argument:

> It is better to be a human being dissatisfied than a pig satisfied; better to be Socrates dissatisfied than a fool satisfied. And if the fool, or the pig, is of a

---

[27] Jeremy Bentham, *The Rationale of Reward*. John Bowring, ed. (Edinburgh: W. Tait; London: Simpkin and Marshall, 1843), book III, ch. I, http://www.laits.utexas.edu/poltheory/bentham/rr/rr.b01.c10.html (accessed 7/4/2016).
[28] Early Utilitarians like Bentham spoke in terms of maximized pleasure; later Utilitarians have broadened this to include needs and wants in general.

different opinion, it is because they only know their own side of the question. The other party to the comparison knows both sides.[29]

This question of quantitative vs. qualitative is not the only issue with which the prospective Utilitarian must wrestle. There is also the choice between "act" and "rule" Utilitarianism. Up to this point I've been talking about Utilitarian choices as if they are always choices between various acts: will we play pushpin or read poetry, will we buy a solidly-built house or several poorly-constructed shanties, will I vote for universal healthcare or against it? This is called "**Act Utilitarianism**" because it focuses on individual actions. But there are problems with this focus. For one thing, when faced with an ethical dilemma, a person often does not have time to make a careful cost-benefit analysis of the various possible courses of action. For another, it can be very difficult to predict the long-term effects of an act. And a focus on acts leaves a person open to the temptation to evaluate acts in a way that is biased by his or her preconceptions and interests.

An alternative is advocated by some Utilitarians: "**Rule Utilitarianism**." This approach involves applying the Utilitarian standard (the greatest good for the most people) to rules of behavior rather than to specific acts. In other words, we should adopt as our moral code those rules of conduct that will result in the greatest good for the most people. This approach has a number of advantages over Act Utilitarianism, particularly to the kind of person who thinks ahead (which is what this book is all about: intentional ethics, remember?). A person who thinks ahead can devise a set of moral precepts by which to guide his actions based

[29] John Stuart Mill, *Utilitarianism.* Roger Crips, ed. (Oxford: Oxford University Press, 1998), 10. In contrast, Mill accused Bentham of holding that "a satisfied pig has equal or more value than a dissatisfied human being."

John Stuart Mill

John Stuart Mill has been called the greatest 19th century British philosopher. His writings on ethics and political theory have been especially influential, but he wrote very widely. He was quite progressive for his day, championing women's suffrage, the abolition of slavery, and the human treatment of animals, among other causes. In his day such positions were considered radical. Today he is best remembered for advocating Utilitarianism in ethics and politics.

Courtesy Library of Congress

on what precepts are likely to most often result in the greatest good for the most people. Then when that person finds himself facing a moral dilemma, he doesn't need to make a cost-benefit analysis of the various courses of action: he merely acts in accord with the moral precept that he has decided on ahead of time.

Another advantage of Rule Utilitarianism is that it increases the distance between the person making the choice and the situation in which he finds himself – it increases objectivity. When you are facing a temptation or a dilemma, it can be difficult to keep your head straight. Emotions, biases, prejudices, personal preferences, and a host of other things come into play that can prevent you from making the right decision. Having a carefully-considered set of moral precepts at hand when facing such a decision may be the only way to see yourself through to the desired outcome. This in fact brings Utilitarianism closer to other ethical theories like Natural Law Theory (chapter four) and Duty Ethics (chapter seven), which also emphasize the importance of having carefully-considered moral principles.

Critical Analysis

I've already mentioned that Utilitarianism feels "right" to many Americans because it resonates with our feeling of solidarity with fellow Americans and our ethos of striving for the betterment of our country. These can be taken as strengths of Utilitarianism, and there are others strengths, too, many of which are very practical. First, in contrast with Ethical Egoism, Utilitarianism strongly encourages consideration for the wellbeing of others. Related to that, it serves as a counterbalance to our natural tendency to put ourselves first.[30] In conjunction with all of these, Utilitarianism engenders strong societies, for the principle at its heart is a principle that is powerfully conducive to social harmony and flourishing. Finally, Utilitarianism seems to be in harmony with the altruistic impulse found in many religions and philosophies. So Utilitarianism has much going for it.

However, there are also quite a few points of concern. It was pointed out in the previous chapter that any sort of consequentialism faces the challenge that it is difficult to accurately predict the long-range consequences of actions. Since Utilitarianism is a form of consequentialism, this is true of Utilitarianism, too. It is especially true of Act Utilitarianism, but to a lesser degree it is true of Rule Utilitarianism as well, for Rule Utilitarianism depends on the ability to accurately predict what the consequences of rules will be.

Many object to Utilitarianism because it, like Ethical Egoism, seems to imply that the ends justifies the means. If the ends really do justify the means, then it seems that it would be possible to justify some truly abhorrent act if it promises (with an appropriate degree of certainty) to bring about the desired end. For example, Americans used to be staunchly opposed to torture, but now many think that torture is justified in some cases because it may help prevent acts of terrorism. This raises a number of questions: were previous generations wrong about torture? If it fails to bring about the anticipated end, was it then immoral? If it's

---

[30] Not everyone agrees that we have such a tendency, of course, but there are a substantial number of people who advocate "**psychological egoism**," which is the view that humans are naturally self-centered. Interestingly, if you combine this view with Ethical Egoism, the result is the view that humans are naturally self-centered and that they ought to be self-centered – which means that humans are naturally inclined to do what they ought to do. Whether this is true is open to debate, of course. Those who reject Ethical Egoism will reject this conclusion out of hand.

sometimes immoral because it fails to bring about the desired end, how can the very same act be moral in other instances?

Finally, and perhaps most fundamentally, there is the objection of the "tyranny of the majority." Why is it that what benefits the most people is always right? If prior to the Civil War slavery benefited the majority of Americans, does that mean it was right? Couldn't it be the case that what benefits the minority over the majority is sometimes right? Couldn't it sometimes be right to do something even if that thing benefits no one, not even the doer? While *prima facie* the standard of "greatest good for the most people" seems ethical, we need more than simply a *prima facie* plausibility if we are going to use this to guide our lives.[31]

Questions to Ponder:

- Ask yourself this: If I were a Utilitarian ethicist, how would I go about determining if an action is moral or immoral?
- What do Ethical Egoism and Utilitarianism have in common, and what distinguishes one from the other?
- Does the observation that we can rarely if ever be certain of the future consequences of our actions fatally undermine Utilitarianism?
- Could it be that the Utilitarian approach to ethics is sometimes appropriate and at other times

---

[31] Rhetorical questions such as these do not constitute arguments against a view, but they do show that there are at least potentially powerful objections to a view. In this case I am not actually arguing that Utilitarianism is false, but rather I am showing that before we can affirm that Utilitarianism is true we have more work to do. In the final analysis I believe that the Utilitarian principle does have a place in our metaethic.

inappropriate? Is there a principled way to tell when it is appropriate and when it is not?

Terms to know:

- Utilitarianism
- Consequentialism
- Act Utilitarianism
- Rule Utilitarianism
- Hedonic Calculus
- Psychological Egoism

For further reading:

- A seminal text on Utilitarianism is John Stuart Mill, *Utilitarianism.* Oxford: Oxford University Press, 1998.
- An influential recent example of Utilitarianism is Peter Singer, *The Expanding Circle: Ethics and Sociobiology.* New York: Farrar, Straus & Giroux, 1981.
- A critique of Utilitarianism is Sterling Harwood, "Eleven Objections to Utilitarianism," in Louis P. Pojman, ed., *Moral Philosophy: A Reader.* Indianapolis, IN: Hackett Publishing Co., 2003.

Chapter Seven

Duty Ethics

Synopsis

In this chapter we will examine the ethical theory of Immanuel Kant, a famous German philosopher. We will begin with his critique of consequentialist approaches to ethics and then explain his alternative and the logic behind it. We will finish with a critical discussion of its strengths and weaknesses.

Introduction

For many of us, when we think about the subject of doing what is morally right, of doing what we ought to do, the term "duty" springs to mind. This is no coincidence, for "oughtness" and "duty" are practically synonyms. The German philosopher Immanuel Kant (1724-1804) saw duty as the central principle of ethics and developed a whole ethical system around it. His system, variously called **"Duty Ethics**," "Kantian Ethics," and "Deontological Ethics," is the subject of this chapter.

Kant had a major problem with consequentialist approaches to ethics like Ethical Egoism and Utilitarianism. He pointed out that such theories are inherently **hypothetical** (also called **conditional**), in the sense that what action is considered right according to the theory depends on which outcome you want to accomplish. In effect, consequentialism says "Do X if you want to accomplish Y." Egoism says "Do X' if you want to be happy, do X'' if you want to live long, do X''' if you want to be popular," etc. Utilitarianism says that you should do whatever produces the most good for the greatest number of people, which translates to "Do X' if it will produce the most good for the most people; if not, then do X'', or X''', or whatever will yield the most good for the most people."

But this renders morality relative to the desired goal (personal happiness, longevity, popularity, or whatever), and that is the path to relativism.

Because of this problem, Kant could not accept a consequentialist metaethic. Let me tell you what he came up with instead.

Theory

Kant was convinced that morality is unconditional; that moral absolutes will be true everywhere, all the time, for everyone. Hence moral principles cannot be conditional statements. They must be unconditional. Because of this they cannot be based upon desired outcomes, for when we base ethics on outcomes, when the desired outcome changes the moral principle will change, too. Nor can they be based on past experiences, for principles that are based on experiences are relative to those experiences. If someone else has had different experiences than you have, then that person will have different principles than you do. Therefore ethical principles must be derived in a totally rational (rather than experiential) way.

A principle that is based on or derived from our experiences is called an *a posteriori* principle. ***A posteriori*** simply means "following from experience." A principle that is derived purely by thinking about it is called *a priori*. ***A priori*** means "preceding experience." The kind of principle that Kant is looking for is *a priori*.

What ethical principle could we possibly formulate without first considering our experiences? At first it might seem like we can't come up with any, because ethics always relates to real-life moral dilemmas that are experiential in nature. But we've already discussed a number of ethical principles that we could conceivably have come up with in an *a priori* fashion. One such

84

Immanuel Kant

Immanuel Kant is perhaps the German philosopher who has had the greatest impact on the English-speaking world. His influence is most keenly felt through his works on epistemology and on ethics. In fact, his epistemology directly impacts his ethics. In his epistemology he basically sides with the Rationalist tradition that says that there can be some significant knowledge apart from the senses. He argues that those things that we know prior to having sensory experiences are necessary prerequisites of intelligible experience. Similarly, in ethics he argues that there is a principle that we know prior to encountering any moral dilemmas and that this principle is what enables us to resolve moral dilemmas. He calls this principle the "categorical imperative."

principle could be that whenever we are faced with a moral dilemma we should follow our common sense, as was discussed in chapter one. Kant would probably reject this approach, though, since common sense is a cultural construct and therefore the results of such an approach would not be true everywhere, all of the time, and for everyone. Another would be that we should always aim for the most balanced position (as discussed in chapter two) – but this is notoriously vague. In politics as well as ethics most people seem to think that their own positions are the most balanced and that disagreeing positions are imbalanced, but since such disagreements involve incommensurable positions, they cannot all be the most balanced at the same time.

A third option would be to allow our conscience to be our guide (as mentioned in chapter three). However, the voice of one's conscience is easily and persistently influenced by one's culture, which implies cultural relativism. Perhaps we should adopt as our guiding principle the maxim that we should always do what is in the best interest of the one making the decision, or the one who must live with the consequences of the action, or whatever is in everyone's best interest. But such consequentialist principles are explicitly rejected by Kant, as has already been explained. Is there any other *a priori* moral principle?

Kant proposes an *a priori* moral principle that he names the "**categorical imperative**." He formulates this in various ways, but the most common version is: "I should never act except in such a way that I can also will that my maxim should become a universal law."[32] What he meant

---

[32] Immanuel Kant, *Grounding for the Metaphysics of Morals, with On a Supposed Right to Lie because of Philanthropic Concerns*, translated by James W. Ellington (Indianapolis, IN: Hackett Publishing Co., 1981), 14. As you have probably already noticed, this principle is very similar to, though not exactly the same as, Jesus' Golden Rule.

by this is that you should accept as the guiding principles of your life only those principles that you wouldn't mind everyone else also living by. For example, if you wouldn't want everyone else living by the principle "It's OK to lie as long as you don't get caught," then you shouldn't, either.

There are very specific reasons that this principle is called the "categorical imperative." It is called an "imperative" because it tells us what we must do in order to act morally. In other words, it tells us what our moral duty is. It is "categorical" in the sense that it is not hypothetical (or conditional). A conditional statement (as explained earlier) says that an action is moral if it leads to desirable results. Its morality is conditioned upon its results. For example, if we want to maximize happiness then we should give people the freedom to look after their own needs (according to Ayn Rand). Hence Rand thinks that a libertarian approach to government is morally justified. In contrast, a categorical statement does not allow the desired ends to determine the means, but instead says that we should act a certain way regardless of what the consequences might be. Kant's imperative is categorical and as a result it tells us what our duty is at all times and in all circumstances. It is, according to Kant, always our duty to live only by principles that we would want others to also live by. If you ever find that you must make yourself a special exception to some principle, that's a good indication that the principle (or the act that it relates to) is not moral. If you wouldn't want others doing it, then you shouldn't do it yourself.

A second way that Kant expresses the categorical imperative is very powerful, so I want to give that to you as well. He calls this the **"practical imperative"**: "Act in such a way that you treat humanity, whether in your own person or in the person of another, always at the same time as an end and never simply as a means."[33] The wording here may make this look like a completely different principle, but at its heart it is fundamentally the same: you are a person with value and rights and want to be treated as such; you should treat others the same way in return.

Why should we think that Kant's principle is any more correct than the others that we've considered? Kant argues that his principle is necessary for rational consistency. Consider this: if you say that it's OK for you to lie but it's not OK for others to lie, then what you are doing is saying that on the one hand lying is moral and on the other hand it is not. So you are saying that lying is both moral and immoral, which is a contradiction. But such a contradiction is illogical, and what is illogical is irrational.[34] Hence adopting a principle that cannot be universalized – cannot be made a principle by which all people should live – leads to irrationality.[35] In other words, the categorical imperative leads to a morality that makes sense and thus to a life that is both morally and rationally consistent.

Critical Analysis

As has been seen, Duty Ethics has some genuine strengths. If Kant is correct, it leads to moral and intellectual

---

[33] Kant, 36.

[34] Christian theologians and some philosophers make use of a distinction between beliefs that are irrational and beliefs that transcend logic. Beliefs such as the Trinity and the incarnation may transcend logic in some ways, but since we have good reasons to believe them, they are not irrational. (What those reasons are is discussed in any standard theology textbook, such as Millard J. Erickson, *Christen Theology*, 3rd edition [Baker Academic, 2013].)

[35] Notice that we are using a *reductio ad absurdum* argument again – how often we make use of this sort of argument!

consistency. It would probably have many practical benefits, too: living by the categorical imperative would help people to get along better, and perhaps it would help nations to get along better, too. It seems like it would help dissolve a very broad range of problems and conflicts. To Christians the categorical imperative may be particularly appealing because of its similarity to the Golden Rule, and it should be mentioned that most religions share a similar precept somewhere in their moral teachings.[36]

However, as a candidate for the foundation of our entire metaethic it faces several challenges. One is that although the principle itself may be objective, both its interpretation and its application seem to be subjective. This is because the task of deciding what maxims everyone should live by is very complex: the judgment about what should be universalized may hinge on subjective elements like preferring excitement over comfort, health over wealth, or liberty over security. For example: one person might want to universalize a libertarian principle of maximal freedom while another might want to universalize a more socialist principle of shared social reasonability. This being the case, how can we possibly adjudicate fairly between these competing preferences?

Another problem is that of conflicting duties. If we have a duty to not infringe on other people's freedom, including their property rights, but we also have a duty to provide for the poor and needy of the world, and if the only way to do so is to redistribute some wealth from the rich to the poor, then we clearly have conflicting duties.

Finally there's the important problem of specificity. How specific should our maxims be? Should the maxim against lying be broad, prohibiting all lying? That's what Kant thought. But how about if telling the simple truth

---

[36] Versions of this precept can be found in Confucianism, Jainism, Buddhism, Zoroastrianism, Hinduism, Judaism, and the Sikh faith, as well as in the writings of various philosophers and elsewhere.

would lead to the death of someone who you are protecting? Perhaps our maxim about lying should be more specific, something more like "Don't lie except when telling the truth would result in someone's death." But of course there could be other similar scenarios in which lying is the lesser of two evils. So perhaps our maxim should be "Don't lie except when doing so is necessary to prevent an even greater evil." But if we form our maxims like this, aren't we then reverting to consequentialism? Aren't we saying that it's immoral to lie if it would bring about the most undesirable result but moral to lie if it would prevent the most undesirable result? Kant would object to this in the same way that he objected to other forms of consequentialism, and his arguments on that subject do seem pretty formidable.

In the final analysis Duty Ethics seems at best partially successful as a metaethic. Hence our search is not over. We need to keep looking.

Questions to Ponder:

- Ask yourself this: If I adopt Duty Ethics as my approach to morality, how would I go about determining if an action is moral or immoral?
- Do you think that the categorical imperative is necessary for rational consistency?
- What does it mean for an act to be "universalized"?
- How is the categorical imperative different from the Golden Rule?
- What is the relationship between our experiences and our moral beliefs?

Terms to know:

- Duty Ethics
- Hypothetical
- Conditional
- Categorical
- *A posteriori*
- *A priori*
- Categorical Imperative
- Practical Imperative

For further reading:

- The starting point for Kantian ethics is Kant's own *Grounding for the Metaphysics of Morals, with On a Supposed Right to Lie because of Philanthropic Concerns*, translated by James W. Ellington. Indianapolis, IN: Hackett Publishing Co., 1981. However, although this book is only a little over 50 pages, it requires slow, thoughtful reading.
- A contemporary defense and exposition of Kant's ethical thought is Onora O'Neill, *Acting on Principle: An Essay on Kantian Ethics*, 2nd ed. Cambridge: Cambridge University Press, 2014.
- A critique of Kantian ethics is Paul Gerard Horrigan, "Critique of Kant's Moral Philosophy," http://www.academia.edu/9966102/Critique_of_Kants _Moral_Philosophy.

Chapter Eight

The Metaphysics of a Christian Ethic

Synopsis

In this chapter we dig into the presuppositions of ethics and find that in order to forge a strong metaethic we must first distinguish between metaphysical questions and epistemological questions. We focus on the metaphysical ones first, saving the epistemological ones for the following chapter. We consider four possible answers to the metaphysical question "What is the underlying nature of moral goodness?" and opt for the fourth answer, which then leads us to pose the epistemological questions that will occupy us in the next chapter.

Introduction

We began our discussion of ethics with a discussion of ethical relativism (chapter two). We saw that if relativism is true, then there are no moral absolutes, but instead what is morally right could and probably will vary from one culture to another. That would have a huge impact on our approach to metaethics, for we would not need to search for absolutes but instead we would focus on what our society currently believes about morality. However, after considering the arguments for and against relativism, we found that the case for relativism is considerably weaker than the case against it. Hence we concluded that relativism is most likely false.

Since relativism is probably false, it follows that there probably are moral absolutes. That being the case, we turned our attention to looking for a way of discovering these absolutes. To this end we discussed a whole range of ethical theories. Although it was never explicitly stated, we have actually been struggling to answer two distinct questions at once: 1. What is the nature of moral goodness?, and 2. How can we know what is morally good? The former question is a metaphysical question. As previously explained, metaphysics is the study of the ultimate nature of reality. The question "What is the nature of moral goodness?" is a metaphysical question because it is asking about the ultimate nature of something (in this case, morality or the moral absolutes).

The latter question is an epistemological question. Epistemology is the theory of knowledge; it deals with how we know things and questions related to belief and truth. The question "How can we know what is morally good?" is an epistemological question because it is asking about how we know something. Hence we're dealing with two very different questions here. Perhaps part of the reason that we've been having difficulty answering them is that we've been trying to answer them both at the same time, as if they are the same question. Maybe it would help if we take them one at a time.

Theory

Let's begin with the metaphysical question. What is "good"? What does the word "good" mean when it is used in moral contexts? Consequentialism, Virtue Ethics, Duty Ethics, and even Natural Law Theory presume some conception of moral goodness, but little has been said about where that conception comes from or whether or not it is correct. These metaethical presuppositions could be very important –and they could be very mistaken, too. Hence we need to turn our attention to examining this important underlying issue.

One theory on the source of our ideas about moral goodness is **Social Contract Theory**. This was perhaps the most influential theory on the origin and nature of morality during the 20th century (though its roots go back to early modern philosophers like Thomas Hobbes [1588-1679], John Locke [1632-1704], and Jean-Jacques Rousseau [1712-1778] and similar suggestions can be found in the ancient works of Plato). Social Contract Theory argues that our idea of what is moral is the result of an implicit agreement between the members of a society that facilitates the functioning of that society. It is like an unwritten contract between you and your neighbors that regulates your responsibilities to each other.

Prima facie this seems like a very reasonable suggestion. There certainly do seem to be a lot of unspoken agreements that help me get along with my neighbors. For example, I like motorcycles and I happen to have three of them. The one that I ride the most is pretty loud – and I kind of like it that way. I enjoy being able to hear each cylinder fire when it's slowly idling, the engine loping along just above a stall. And I like the sound it makes when I'm powering through a curve – the honk of the intake through the carbs that I've tuned myself, the powerful rumble of the exhaust from which I've removed some of the baffles… But I'm very aware of the fact that not everyone shares this pleasure. In fact, hearing my motorcycle roar up and down our hill could be very annoying to our neighbors, very few of whom are motorcycle aficionados. Hence I stay off the throttle most of the time, especially early in the morning and late at night. My neighbors have never said anything to me about the sound of my motorcycles annoying them, mind you, but that's because they don't need to: I've already taken care of the problem through exercising self-control.

When we think about the idea behind Social Contract Theory this way, it seems to be rather common-sense. And in fact it is, if you remember the explanation of common sense given in the first chapter of this book. There it was argued that common sense is largely a social

Thomas Hobbes

Thomas Hobbes was an English political theorist whose book *Leviathan* develops an early example of Social Contract Theory. He argues that by nature humans are in competition and conflict with each other, a situation that would inevitably lead to abuse and in some cases death if not somehow mitigated. In order to survive and prosper, people form cooperative communities wherein each member implicitly recognizes and respects the needs of others. This is the so-called "social contract" and is seen by Hobbes as the source of social ethics.

©Georgios Kollidas/Shutterstock.com

source of knowledge. Social Contract Theory is positing just that: our moral beliefs are a social construct, created by cultures, often over long periods of time, and they are culturally relative. In fact, Social Contract Theory fits quite nicely with cultural relativism.

It makes sense to say that our ideas about what is right and what is wrong reflect, at least to a very significant extent even if not completely, the implicit beliefs of our culture. However, inasmuch as this is basically a form of cultural relativism, it is subject to all of the objections that cultural relativism is. And there is a further significant objection to Social Contract Theory. Social Contract Theory says that each society has its own social contract, and that the contract of one society may differ significantly from that of another. Critics of Social Contract Theory point out that it seems to be at least theoretically possible to compare the social contracts of various societies and evaluate which contracts are the most restrictive, the most permissive, the most fair, the most just, etc. But some of these categories are clearly moral categories, and the conclusions drawn in this evaluation will be, at least in part, moral conclusions. In short, it can be determined which social contract is the best, morally speaking. If that's the case, though, then there must be a conception of moral goodness that is over and above the social contracts being compared, some moral standard to which they can be held. Social Contract Theory does not really explain where this concept of the good comes from. Thus while Social Contract Theory seems partially correct, it cannot be the final explanation of the source of the good.

An alternative to Social Contract Theory is **Divine Command Theory**. Many theistic ethicists have held that what is good is good because God commands it. They reason that since God is the source of all things, he must also be the source of morals, too. Furthermore, they reason that since God is sovereign and omnipotent, he has both the

John Locke

Following Hobbes' lead, the English philosopher and physician John Locke also argued for a sort of Social Contract Theory. He saw the authority of the government as coming from the consent of the governed via the (unspoken) social contract. This idea greatly influenced the founding fathers of the United States of America. Locke also believed that each human has certain inalienable rights that are bestowed on him or her by God. Because these are unalienable, they should not be surrendered in favor of the social contract nor should government attempt to infringe upon them.

J. LOCKE

Courtesy Library of Congress

authority and the power to decide what will be morally right and what will be morally wrong. According to traditional Divine Command Theory, loving your neighbor is good simply because God commands it; murder is evil simply because God has prohibited it. And this is true for the rest of morality, too: God determines what is right and wrong, good and bad.

Many of my readers probably empathize with this view. Many of you are probably Christians (or theists of some other sort) who share this high view of God as creator and ruler of all. I view God that way, too. However, there are serious challenges to Divine Command Theory, challenges that even a devout Christian should recognize.

The heart of the problem with Divine Command Theory was hinted at long ago, in a story told by the ancient Greek philosopher Plato. In his book *Euthyphro* Plato has his teacher, Socrates, enter into a discussion about the nature and source of morality with a young man named Euthyphro who he meets on his way to court. Euthyphro is prosecuting his own father for causing the death of a slave. Socrates seems surprised that someone would prosecute his own father and wants to understand why Euthyphro thinks it morally right to do so. So Socrates askes Euthyphro a series of questions leading to the following discussion of the nature and source of morality:

Euthyphro: Piety, then, is that which is dear to the gods, and impiety is that which is not dear to them.
Socrates: There was a notion that came into my mind while you were speaking; I said to myself: "Well, and what if Euthyphro does prove to me that all the gods regarded the death of the serf as unjust, how do I know anything more of the nature of piety and impiety? for granting that this action may be hateful to the gods, still piety and impiety are not adequately defined by these distinctions, for that which is hateful to the gods has been shown to be also

pleasing and dear to them." And therefore, Euthyphro, I do not ask you to prove this; I will suppose, if you like, that all the gods condemn and abominate such an action. But I will amend the definition so far as to say that what all the gods hate is impious, and what they love pious or holy; and what some of them love and others hate is both or neither. Shall this be our definition of piety and impiety?

Euthyphro: Yes, I should say that what all the gods love is pious and holy, and the opposite which they all hate, impious.

Socrates: The point which I should first wish to understand is whether the pious or holy is beloved by the gods because it is holy, or holy because it is beloved of the gods.[37]

The last line poses what has famously become known as the "**Euthyphro Dilemma.**" It is called a dilemma because regardless of which of the possibilities Euthyphro opts for he will find himself in a bad place. If he chooses the first option – that something is beloved by the gods because it is holy – then he has the problem that holiness is something that exists independently of the will of the gods. This is a problem because if being holy is what causes the gods to love something, then the fact that the gods love it does not explain why it is holy. On the other hand, if he opts for the second possibility – that whatever is holy is holy because it is loved by the Gods – then he implies that anything that the gods love would be holy. This is a problem because it makes holiness arbitrary, the result being that anything could be holy depending on the whims of the (often fickle) Greek gods.

Don't be distracted by the obvious polytheism in this passage. The issues that Plato (via Socrates) points out are challenges to a monotheistic Divine Command Theory

---

[37] The complete text of Plato's *Euthyphro* can be read online at http://classics.mit.edu/Plato/euthyfro.html.

Plato

Plato is perhaps the most important figure aside from Jesus in the whole Western intellectual tradition. He lived in Athens when Greece was the intellectual center of the Western world. He was a student of Socrates and the teacher of Aristotle. The extent of his influence is reflected in one philosopher's remark that the history of Western philosophy is a series of footnotes to Plato. One reason why he has been so tremendously influential is probably that his writings, which are usually in the form of dialogues between Socrates and other Athenians, are much more readable than are the writings of most great intellectuals.

©zebra0209/Shutterstock.com

just as much as to a polytheistic one. Many contemporary ethicists, skeptical of the feasibility of Divine Command Theory, have posed challenges like, "Is what is moral determined by the will of God, or is God's will determined by what is moral?"

Do you see the dilemma here? If we say that God's will determines what is moral, then we imply that nothing is inherently immoral, with the result that God could choose to make anything at all moral. This is a problem for several reasons, including that it makes morality arbitrary, that it deprives us of any sort of explanation for why God chooses one thing to be moral instead of another, and that if true, then things like torturing innocent little children merely for the fun of it could be moral if God so chooses (which seems highly improbable to many people).

On the other hand, if we say that God's will is determined by what is moral – in other words, that there is a standard of morality that exists independent from God and to which God's will must conform in order to be moral – then we cause ourselves at least two problems. First, we are saying that there is a moral authority higher than God, which seems to impugn God's sovereignty. Second, we fail to answer the question of the source of morality, for saying "God's will is determined by what is moral" does not explain how "what is moral" got to be moral in the first place.

A possible solution to some of the problems of Divine Command Theory is the view that is called **Moral Realism**. Moral realists believe that moral principles are an immaterial part of reality that exist even though they cannot be seen or felt, similar to the laws of logic and the laws of nature, each of which are real even though they are not physical. Some moral realists are naturalists and believe that moral principles are simple "brute facts" that are not predicated upon anything else. Others are theists who believe that moral principles exist apart from God, and that

God's commands conform to them because God, being omniscient, has perfect knowledge of them, and being holy, perfectly abides by them.[38] According to this view, ethical absolutes really do exist, and they exist independently of any being, human or divine. This view dates back as far as Plato and fits well with ethical absolutism. I would estimate that most Americans who are not relativists are probably Moral Realists.

Despite its popularity, Moral Realism faces some fairly serious objections. For the theist, an important objection is that this view makes God subject to something outside of himself, which seems to impugn his sovereignty. For both the theist and the non-theist there is the problem that Moral Realism does not provide an explanation of where moral principles come from, how they came about, why they exist, or anything like that. (The way ethicists who are critical of Moral Realism express this is that Moral Realism lacks "explanatory power.") The naturalistic moral realist asserts that moral principles are brute facts, but the justification for this assertion is simply that no better explanation is available. However, I think that there is a better explanation for morality, so let's look at one more option.

Recently some theistic ethicists have argued for a **modified Divine Command Theory** that some are calling **Divine Nature Theory**.[39] These thinkers suggest that a better solution to the problems of Divine Command Theory would be to view moral principles as a reflection of the

---

[38] The book *God & Morality: Four Views* contains chapters defending atheistic Moral Realism and theistic Moral Realism as well as atheistic moral constructivism and modified Divine Command Theory. *God & Morality: Four Views*, R. Keith Loftin, ed. (Downers Gove, IL: IVP Academic, 2012).

[39] One influential figure in this movement is the theistic ethicists Robert Adams, who has taught philosophy at UCLA, Yale, and other leading schools in the USA and Great Britain. See the Further Readings section of this chapter for information on one of his books.

ultimate good that is inherent in the nature of God himself. They argue that God's commands do not determine what is good, but rather they institutionalize and communicate the good that is part of the unchanging nature of God. If this is the case, then moral principles are not arbitrary. Nor are they relative, cultural constructs. Instead, what is good is a reflection of the ultimate nature of reality, because ultimately reality is God and his actions.

This theory combines elements of Divine Command Theory and Moral Realism. It does so in a way that shows the Euthyphro Dilemma to be a false dilemma, for there is a workable third option. Divine Nature Theory denies that morality is arbitrarily determined by God's choices, for if morality reflects the unchanging nature of God, then no choice is necessary in order to determine what is right. Thus it overcomes the arbitrariness objection. And it rejects the suggestion that there is a standard of morality outside of God to which God's commands conform, for now the standard is internal to God – in effect, God is the standard. Furthermore it overcomes the "no explanatory power" objection to Moral Realism, for it provides an explanation of the source of morality, one that is far more satisfying than a mere assertion of "brute fact" if you grant the existence of God.

The main objection to Divine Nature Theory is that it is dependent on the existence of God, which is a belief that many no longer share. This is true, though of course many people do still believe in God. But the fact that many people don't believe something doesn't prove it false.

Conclusion

In this chapter we have examined a number of possible answers to the metaphysical question: "What is the source or nature of moral goodness?" I have argued that moral goodness is a reflection of or aspect of the nature of God. This is my answer to the underlying metaphysical question that we've been wrestling with since the second chapter of this book. It's nice to finally have an answer!

However, this particular answer is problematic, for it has the potential to make it difficult to answer the second of our questions, the epistemological one: "How can we know what is morally good?" If morality is an aspect or reflection of God's nature, and if God's nature transcends human understanding (God is thought by many to be much greater than what our little human minds can comprehend), then how can we possibly know what the good is? Can we wrap our minds around morality if we can't wrap our minds around the nature of God? These are obviously epistemological questions. Perhaps we need to restart our metaethics by doing some meta-metaethics: the question of ethical epistemology.

Questions to Ponder:
- What is the difference between a metaphysical question and an epistemological one?
- What is the underlying nature of moral goodness? What is it about an act that makes it moral or immoral?
- Social Contract Theory seems to be a form of Ethical Relativism. What other metaethical theories is it similar to?
- Divine Command Theory and Moral Realism are both non-relativistic theories. How do they differ from each other?
- How does Divine Command Theory differ from Divine Nature Theory?
- How is Divine Nature Theory epistemologically problematic?

Terms to know:
Social Contract Theory
Divine Command Theory
The Euthyphro Dilemma
Moral Realism
Divine Nature Theory
Modified Divine Command Theory

For further reading:
- Anyone interested in Divine Command Theory in any of its forms should read Plato's *Euthyphro*. There are many published translations and it can be found for free on the internet. This is not a difficult read.
- A popular article showing the connection between morality and the nature of God is William Lane Craig, "The Indispensability of Theological Meta-ethical Foundations for Morality," Afterall.net. http://afterall.net/papers/the-indispensability-of-theological-meta-ethical-foundations-for-morality/ (accessed June 27, 2017).
- An important thinker in the contemporary Modified Divine Command Theory tradition is Robert Adams. One of his books on this subject is *Finite and Infinite Goods: A Framework for Ethics*. Oxford: Oxford University Press, 2002.
- Another recent book in the Modified Divine Command Theory tradition is David Baggett and Jerry Walls, *Good God: The Theistic Foundations of Morality*. Oxford: Oxford University Press, 2011.
- A readable introduction to competing theories on the underlying nature of moral principles is R. Keith Loftin, ed., *God and Morality: Four Views*. Downers Grove, IL: IVP Academic, 2012.

Chapter Nine

The Epistemology of a Christian Ethic

Synopsis

In this chapter we continue developing a Christian metaethic. Building on the metaphysical foundation developed in the previous chapter, we delve into the epistemology of a Christian approach to ethics, emphasizing the role of divine revelation but eventually also returning to the previously-discussed philosophical ethical theories, finding value in many of them when placed within the framework of a Christian ethic. Along the way we discuss how to interpret the Bible accurately and the logic used in applying the Bible to issues in applied ethics.

Introduction

In the previous chapter we saw that a cogent answer to the fundamental question "What is the nature and source of moral goodness?" is that moral goodness is an aspect or reflection of the nature of God, who is perfectly good.[40] However, this answer to our metaphysical question about the nature of morality leads us to a similarly fundamental epistemological question: How can we know what is morally good? This could be a vexing question, for if morality is an aspect or reflection of God's nature, and if God's nature transcends human understanding, then how can we possibly know what the good is?

An epistemologist is someone who studies how people gain knowledge, what knowledge is, and similar

---

[40] Good discussions of why moral goodness is a fundamental aspect of the nature of God are found in Thomas Morris, *Our Idea of God: An Introduction to Philosophical Theology* (Vancouver: Regent College Publishing, 1991) 47-64, and David Baggett and Jerry L. Walls. *Good God: The Theistic Foundations of Morality* (NY: Oxford University Press, 2011) chapter 5, "God and Goodness."

issues. Epistemologists have identified a range of approaches to knowledge acquisition and belief justification, including versions of rationalism, empiricism, intuitionism, foundationalism, and others. Each of the metaethical theories that we have discussed implicitly or explicitly utilizes some such approach to knowledge acquisition. For example, consequentialist metaethical theories do not appeal to intuition or abstract rationality but rather to experience, making inferences from past experiences to conclusions about the likely results of actions or rules, and as such they are employing an empiricist epistemology. Kantian Duty Ethics, on the other hand, is intentionally rationalist, for Kant believes that the categorical imperative is discovered through an abstract, rational contemplation of morality.

Neither consequentialism nor Duty Ethics was ultimately successful in building a satisfactory ethical system. This suggests that the epistemological strategies underlying these metaethics (empiricism and rational empiricism, respectively) are not the best epistemology by which to approach ethics. What epistemology should we use, then? That is the subject of this chapter.[41]

Theory

Since morality is a reflection of the nature of God, it makes at least *prima facie* sense that we would apply the same epistemology in ethics that we would apply when doing theology. How would you expect to gain knowledge about the nature or God? Many theologians, past and present, believe that we can only have knowledge of God if he

---

[41] A very readable introduction to epistemology is James K. Dew Jr. and Mark W. Foreman, *How Do We Know?: An Introduction to Epistemology* (Downers Grove, IL: IVP Academic, 2014).

reveals himself to us. This could be true for ethics as well. A revelational approach to ethics would fit extremely well with the position that morality is a reflection of the holy nature of a transcendent God who himself can only be known through his self-revelation.

This naturally leads to the question "Has God revealed himself, and does this revelation include an ethical system, or at least the foundational principles necessary for constructing an ethical system?" Theologians argue that God has revealed himself in a number of ways, and theistic ethicists believe that God has revealed foundational ethical principles as well as applications of these principles.

These positions do not need to be taken on blind faith. Theistic scholars have worked diligently to show that there are good reasons for believing in God and divine revelation.[42] One fruitful line of argumentation begins with the historicity of the resurrection of Jesus of Nazareth.

Scholarly historical research has shown that there is very solid evidential support for belief in Jesus' resurrection.[43] Gary Habermas has argued cogently that this resurrection cannot be a natural event, hence there must exist a supernatural power; that this power is best understood as a personal God; and that the resurrection places God's stamp of approval on the life and teachings of the one resurrected. Hence Jesus' life and teachings are approved by God. Since truthfulness is part of God's

---

[42] A very interesting and readable book on these issues is Gregory A. Boyd and Edward K. Boyd's autobiographical *Letters from a Skeptic: A Son Wrestles with his Father's Questions about Christianity* (Wheaton, IL: Victor Books, 1994). A more academic volume is Douglas Groothuis, *Christian Apologetics: A Comprehensive Case for Biblical Faith* (Downers Grove, IL: IVP Academic, 2011).

[43] See, for example, Michael R. Licona, *The Resurrection of Jesus: A New Historiographical Approach* (Downers Grove, IL: IVP Academic, 2010) and N. T. Wright, *The Resurrection of the Son of God* (Minneapolis, MN: Fortress Press, 2003).

Habermas' 12 Widely-Accepted Facts

The American historian and philosopher Gary Habermas provides a list of 12 facts accepted by most historians that, when put together, strongly support the belief that Jesus of Nazareth was miraculously resurrected.

1. Jesus died by crucifixion.
2. He was buried.
3. His death caused the disciples to despair and lose hope.
4. The tomb was empty (this is the most contested of the 12).
5. The disciples had experiences which *they believed* were literal appearances of the risen Jesus.
6. The disciples were transformed from doubters to bold proclaimers.
7. The resurrection was the central message of the early church.
8. The message of Jesus' resurrection was preached in Jerusalem.
9. Christianity was born and grew.
10. Orthodox Jews who believed in Christ made Sunday their primary day of worship.
11. James had been skeptical but was converted to Christianity when he saw the resurrected Jesus.
12. The Pharisee Saul was converted to Christianity and became the Apostle Paul when he encountered the resurrected Jesus.

Habermas' work can be found on his website: www.garyhabermas.com

nature, God would not approve of Jesus' teachings if they are substantially false. Hence Jesus' teachings should be accepted as true.

One of the things that Jesus taught was that the Hebrew Bible was revealed by God. Thus we arrive at the conclusion that God has revealed himself through the Hebrew Bible. Furthermore, since the Hebrew Bible contains many ethical principles and applications, we can affirm that God's revelation includes ethical data that can be used in forming an ethical system. Habermas extends this argument to include the New Testament by showing that Jesus anticipated that the apostles would preserve and pass on his teachings and that the apostles viewed their writings as scripture.[44]

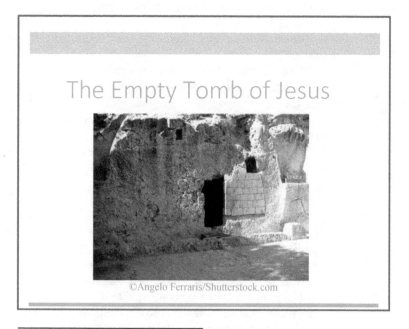

The Empty Tomb of Jesus

©Angelo Ferraris/Shutterstock.com

---

[44] This argument is found in Gary R. Habermas, *The Risen Jesus and Future Hope* (New York: Rowman & Littlefield, 2003). Oliver O'Donavan explicitly connects the resurrection to ethics in *Resurrection and Moral Order: An Outline for Evangelical Ethics* 2nd edition (Grand Rapids: Eerdmans, 1994).

Hermeneutics

The question that follows for us is, "How should the Bible be used in ethics?" The answer is less obvious and much more detailed than some would expect. Many Christians seem to think that the Bible is a plain and simple book of moral and religious sayings the meaning of which is, in general, fairly obvious. There is some truth here – a smidgeon. An average person can study and understand the Bible; an advanced degree in theology is not required. But the Bible is not some middle-school piece of literature: it is a collection of writings that were composed over a long expanse of time by people with a variety of backgrounds who were communicating some pretty advanced religious and philosophical ideas. In order to understand what the authors are trying to communicate we need to read it in a manner that is hermeneutically informed.

Hermeneutics is the science of accurately interpreting difficult texts. If your goal is to uncover the original message of the author (called "**authorial intent**"), then what you are trying to do is called "exegesis." **Exegesis** is the process of drawing out of a text its original meaning. The opposite of exegesis is **eisegesis**, which is the process of reading ideas or an interpretation into a text instead of drawing out of the text the authorial intent.

The most reliable way to perform an exegesis of a biblical text is to utilize a **grammatical-historical-contextual hermeneutic**. That sounds much more intimidating than it actually is. Let me break it down into parts for you. "Grammatical" refers to the language of the text you are reading. If you want to uncover the authorial intent, you need to pay close attention to the actual words that the author uses, trying to understand them as they were used in the day that the text was originally written. Most of the Bible was written in Hebrew and Greek, but those who do not know these ancient languages can learn much about the meaning of the original words by using Bible commentaries, the indices in Strong's Concordance, Vine's Expository Dictionary of New Testament Words, and other such secondary sources.[45] Paying attention to the author's language does not stop at the words; in fact, that is just the beginning. We also need to pay attention to how he puts the words together – what phrases, idioms, metaphors, and other figures of speech he uses when trying to communicate his message, which he probably views as being urgently important – with conviction and persuasiveness.

"Historical" refers to the historical context in which the text was written. Quite often a knowledge of the times in which a text is written and the religious, cultural, political climate of that era will shed new light on a text. For example, if someone were to try to understand the New Testament who has no knowledge of the Hebrew Bible, much of what she would read would seem strange and would be confusing, for much of the New Testament is based on and reflects the events, teachings, and revelations contained in the Hebrew Bible. Sometimes readers of the New Testament who are fairly familiar with the Hebrew Bible seem to forget that the history recorded therein forms a significant aspect of the historical context of the New Testament and as a result they misinterpret parts of the New Testament. An example of this is the reading of Hebrews 11:1 ("Now faith is the substance of things hoped for, the evidence of things not seen.") that interprets this passage as defining faith as believing in God without evidence. Many of the examples of faith provided in verses three through 40 are examples of people in the Hebrew

---

[45] James Strong, *The New Strong's Expanded Exhaustive Concordance of the Bible* (Grand Rapids, MI: Thomas Nelson Publishing Co., 2010); W. E. Vine, *Vine's Expository Dictionary of the Old and New Testament Words* (Grand Rapids, MI: Thomas Nelson Publishing Co., 2003).

Bible who experienced God and then learned to trust in him, so the term "faith" in the first verse of the chapter is not likely to have such a fideistic meaning.[46]

"Contextual" refers to the literary context in which the text is found. Perhaps the most common mistake people make when using the Bible is to take verses out of their context. Always check the context of the verses that you think support your position! When checking the context you usually need to read the whole paragraph in which the verse occurs in order to get a broader understanding of what the author is talking about before you can be sure what he is addressing in the particular verse that you are studying. It's not uncommon for me to read several paragraphs, amounting to a chapter or two of the Bible, in order to follow a writer's train of thought leading up to the verse that I'm trying to interpret.

An additional aspect of "literary context" is the literary genre in which the verse occurs. When trying to exegete a passage it is very helpful to be aware of the type of literature you are reading. If you are reading history, for example, the degree of literalness of the message will be much higher than if you are reading poetry. (There are some books in the Bible that are almost completely history, while the book of Psalms is almost completely poetic.) Poetic, prophetic, and apocalyptic literature contain much more symbolism than do the gospels and the epistles of the New Testament, but those contain more symbolism than do the historical books. And within individual books it is good to be aware that the author can utilizes a variety of literary styles, such as parables, analogies, and metaphors.

I cannot overstate how important it is to pay close attention to the historical and literary context when you are

---

[46] Fideism is the view that faith is a form of belief that does not derive its justification from supporting evidence. It is, in essence, the view that faith is a result of an act of the will.

interpreting the Bible. As they say in hermeneutics, "context is king!"[47]

Logic

More remains to be said about the Bible and ethics. I still need to explain how the carefully-interpreted Bible is useful in responding to ethical dilemmas. When we think about the logic behind applying the Bible to ethical dilemmas, those who are versed in logic see at least three different ways that this can be done.

The most obvious way to use the Bible in ethics is to seek passages that directly address the moral issue that you are facing. The Bible contains many commands, prohibitions, proverbs, exhortations, and the like that give us direction on how to live morally, ranging from the Ten Commandments given early in the Hebrew Bible to the warning at the end of the Book of Revelation not to add to the prophecies contained therein.[48]

However, the Bible provides more than a simple "list metaethic" – much more. And that's an important point. For the number of commands and prohibitions contained in the Bible, though large, is considerably smaller than the number of moral dilemmas that you could conceivably face in your lifetime. So how would you proceed if you were faced by a moral dilemma that you cannot find dealt with in a direct way in the Bible?

---

[47] This is an extremely brief summary of a few basic hermeneutical principles. For those who have never studied hermeneutics, I highly recommend reading an introductory hermeneutics textbook like Andreas J. Köstenberger and Richard Patterson, *Invitation to Biblical Interpretation: Exploring the Hermeneutical Triad of History, Literature, and Theology* (Grand Rapids, MI: Kregel Academic & Professional, 2011).
[48] Revelation 22:18, 19

When the Bible does not address an issue directly, another way to use the Bible as a resource for ethics is to seek general principles in the Bible from which you can deduce conclusions about things that are not addressed directly.[49] Preachers do this all the time, though often they are not aware that this is what they are doing. Any time you argue that the Bible teaches that in situation X you should do Y, the situation you are facing is a type of X, and therefore you should do Y, you are doing exactly what I am describing.

An example of this is the advice often presented to teens by youth pastors. Youth workers often exhort young people in their congregations not to date unbelievers. Sometimes they go as far as to say that the Bible commands believers not to date (or marry) unbelievers. That may be an overstatement, though. First of all, there is a legitimate hermeneutical question about taking commands that were specifically given to Israel and applying them to people outside of Israel, Christian or otherwise. We should not blithely ignore the context in which those commands were originally given. If by some legitimate theological or hermeneutical principles the command can be applied to non-Israelites, that's fine, but only in the presence of such a principle should that ever be done.

Youth leaders are on less difficult ground when they support their message with a New Testament passage directed to Christians. Here the most commonly-used passage is II Corinthians 6:14, where the Apostle Paul writes, "Be ye not unequally yoked together with unbelievers: for what fellowship hath righteousness with

---

[49] **Deduction** is a way of reasoning that works by showing that a conclusion follows from the evidence in a logically necessary, unavoidable way. Deductive arguments lead to conclusions that are just as true as the evidence that supports them because of the close logical relationship between the evidence and the conclusion.

unrighteousness?" The problem with this passage is that, when read in its context, it is not talking about dating at all. Paul's primary concern seems to be that the church in Corinth be a pure congregation, not accepting into their assembly those who are not true believers. It's an ecclesiastical issue, not a dating issue. But when we look at Paul's argument more closely, we see that he takes a general principle, "Be ye not unequally yoked together with unbelievers," and applies this to the particular issue that he is facing. Hence this passage provides us with both a general principle and an example of an application of the principle. The principle itself can be applied to issues other than the one that Paul was facing. One such issue is dating unbelievers.

In short, while this passage is not talking about dating, the principle that it contains can legitimately be applied to dating, as well as to church membership, business relationships, and any other situation that could involve a Christian being "yoked" to an unbeliever in a way that would be problematic. When a youth worker uses this passage to advocate that those under his or her ministry not date unbelievers, the logic of the application is deductive:

1. If you date an unbeliever then you are unequally yoked to that person.
2. The Bible says not to be unequally yoked.
3. Therefore you should not date an unbeliever.[50]

There are many other general principles in the Bible. Examples include the Shema, the Ten Commandments, the Golden Rule, and Paul's teaching that the body is the temple of the Holy Spirit. Principles like

---

[50] The logical form of this argument is called modus tollens or "denying the antecedent."

these can be used for guidance in a wide range of situations.

How will you proceed, though, if you find yourself facing a moral dilemma that isn't directly addressed in the Bible and for which you are having difficulty finding a general principle that could be applied to it without twisting the principle and distorting it beyond recognition? There is at least one more way that we can use the Bible for guidance, and this time it involves inductive rather than deductive logic. If there is a situation in the Bible that is parallel to the situation that you are facing, then you can reason to a conclusion about how you should respond to your situation by comparing it to the Biblical situation and how the biblical character(s) responded. Here you will be using **analogous induction**, which is a form of reasoning that compares two things that are similar in many ways in order to make a judgement about the likeliness that they are similar in other ways, too.[51]

It is easier to illustrate how this works than to explain it. Happily, the Bible contains many examples of analogous induction. One comes from the Apostle Paul's response to an issue that he addresses in the ninth chapter of I Corinthians. Apparently there was a controversy in the Corinthian church about whether a person should be paid for ministry performed. This would apply to apostles, like Paul, and also to other ministers, be they pastors, missionaries, or something else. The argument that Paul provides in support of his position – that ministers should be paid for the work they do – is a bit surprising, but it's clearly based on an analogy between his problem and a

---

[51] Inductive reasoning is a form of logical thought where evidence is used to show that some conclusion is likely to be true, even if it can't be know with complete certainty that it is true. **Induction** is the sort of logic most often used in historical research and is also often used in science.

situation in the Hebrew Bible. The heart of his argument is found in verses nine and ten:

> For it is written in the law of Moses, Thou shalt not muzzle the mouth of the ox that treadeth out the corn. Doth God take care for oxen? Or saith he it altogether for our sakes? For our sakes, no doubt, this is written: that he that ploweth should plow in hope; and that he that thresheth in hope should be partaker of his hope.

Here Paul sees that there is an important parallel between an ox that labors for its owner and a minister who labors in the gospel. He infers that, even as God cares about the ox being rewarded and deriving sustenance from his labor, so should the minister be rewarded sustenance because of his labor in the ministry and be encouraged in his labor by receiving sustenance through it.

This analogy is a bit of a surprise, but it's a legitimate argument, and it serves as a fine example of analogous induction in Christian applied ethics. Other, less surprising examples can be found in the Bible. Many times the New Testament uses passages in the Hebrew Bible in a way that is essentially analogous induction (though it often has to do with spiritual rather than moral issues).[52]

Philosophical Metaethics Revisited

At the heart of the Christian metaethic that I have been developing lies the idea of revelation. It is a metaethic of

---

[52] Another example is Jesus' use of I Samuel 21:1-6, which records David taking shewbread from the tabernacle in order to feed his men, to show that it is acceptable for his disciples to shell and eat grain on the Sabbath, as is recorded in Luke 2:23-28.

Christian revelation. As such it is essentially theological. But what about all of those philosophical metaethical theories that we discussed in chapters three through seven – are they of no value? Did we examine them merely to see that philosophical ethics fails and must be replaced by theology? Definitely not!

There is quite a bit of value in the philosophical approaches to ethics that we have studied. In fact, most of the theories that we discussed reflect principles that we can find in the Bible but might not have noticed had not the philosophers brought them to our attention. Allow me to elaborate.

The heart of Virtue Ethics is the insight that what we do flows from who we are and therefore we need to cultivate a virtuous character if we are going to respond to situations morally. Although Aristotle didn't get this insight from the Bible, it is a very biblical idea. Consider the words of Jesus in Matthew 12:34, 35, "…out of the abundance of the heart the mouth speaketh. A good man out of the good treasure of the heart bringeth forth good things: and an evil man out of the evil treasure bringeth forth evil things." His language is even stronger in Matthew 15:17-20, "Do not ye yet understand, that whatsoever entereth in at the mouth goeth into the belly, and is cast out into the draught? But those things which proceed out of the mouth come forth from the heart; and they defile the man. For out of the heart proceed evil thoughts, murders, adulteries, fornications, thefts, false witness, blasphemies: These are the things which defile a man: but to eat with unwashen hands defileth not a man." In harmony with Jesus' teaching that our actions follow from our essence is Paul's exhortation to therefore cultivate a Godly character in I Timothy 4: 7, 8, "…train yourself to be godly. For physical training is of some value, but godliness has value for all things, holding promise for both the present life and the life to come."[53]

Another aspect of Virtue Ethics is the idea of looking to a virtuous role model in order to determine how to respond to complex moral dilemmas. One problem with this suggestion is that no mere human role model is completely above reproach. Furthermore, selection of the right role model could be rather subjective. But Jesus provides us with the ultimate role model, since he is the God-man, as perfectly moral as God the Father. The sometimes-derided bumper sticker slogan "WWJD" is actually a very good guide to morality!

Turning our attention to Duty Ethics, the similarity between Kant's Categorical Imperative ("I should never act except in such a way that I can also will that my maxim should become a universal law"[54]) and Jesus' Golden Rule ("as ye would that men should do to you, do ye also to them likewise"[55]) can hardly be missed. Both are implying that you should treat others as you would want to be treated, though Kant's version is rule-oriented while Jesus' appears more focused on acts, and Jesus' version also seems more individualistic than Kant's. But affirming that a person ought to give such thought to the rules by which she guides her life complements the idea that she should treat others as she would want to be treated. There is a complementarity between these principles rather than a competition. Duty ethics compliments the Golden Rule. Since the heart of both principles is the same (even though the argument that Kant provided for his principle is not found in the Bible), it can be affirmed that the Categorical

---

[53] *New American Standard Bible* (La Habra, CA: The Lockman Foundation, 1995).

[54] Kant, 14.

[55] Luke 6:31. In the Jewish tradition this principle is first found in Leviticus 19:18 and is reiterated in other Jewish sources prior to and following Jesus.

Imperative is at its heart a biblical principle, and it can be argued that the Categorical Imperative sheds light on implications of the Golden Rule that we might otherwise miss.

Utilitarianism is an approach to ethics that *prima facie* seems to fit well with the spirit of Christianity. After all, didn't Jesus sacrifice himself for the wellbeing of all humanity, one man being killed for the salvation of many? Wasn't that doing what would bring about the greatest good for the most people? However, some Christian thinkers are very uncomfortable with any sort of consequentialism. As Kant pointed out, this does introduce an element of relativism into ethics, for what is right according to consequentialism (be it Utilitarianism or Egoism) is relative to the consequences. Would we really want to say that it is moral to kill an innocent person if the consequences would benefit a great many other people? Although Jesus gave his life willingly, we must bear in mind that the Bible condemns Judas for betraying him and bringing about his death. The Bible does not portray Judas' betrayal as a good deed, despite the enormously beneficial results stemming from it (propitiation and reconciliation between God and humanity, for instance). Hence it is not transparently clear that Jesus' death actually provides a basis for an argument for Utilitarianism.

However, there are examples of what appears to be consequentialist reasoning and consequentialist justification in the Bible. For example, the eighth chapter of Joshua records the Israelites' capture of the city Ai. Their first attempt was a failure; their second attempt succeeds because God gives them a battle plan that involves deceiving the city's defenders into thinking that the Israelites are retreating so that the defenders will pursue the Israelites and leave the city defenseless. Then other Israelites who are in hiding attack and conquer Ai. This passage raises interesting ethical and theological questions.

If God is perfectly holy, how could he be the instigator of such deception? Isn't deception sinful?

The Bible does affirm that God is perfectly holy.[56] Philosophical arguments support this conclusion as well.[57] In this passage God appears to be commanding (and hence condoning) an immoral act, but that interpretation of the passage is not consistent with the ancient Hebrew view of God and the biblical conception of God and hence it is not likely to be the correct interpretation of the passage. A more likely alternative is that God considers deception justified in certain contexts, including in war.[58] Why would deception be justified in war? Perhaps because it is necessary to achieve the needed outcome, which in this case is the victory of the Israelites over Ai.

There are other examples of consequentialist reasoning in the Hebrew Bible, but let us turn to the New Testament. Matthew 7:15-20 records Jesus warning his followers about false teachers. He says,

---

[56] Many passages affirm this, such as Isaiah 6:3, "And one cried unto another, and said, Holy, holy, holy, is the LORD of hosts: the whole earth is full of his glory" and Revelation 4:8, "And the four beasts had each of them six wings about him; and they were full of eyes within: and they rest not day and night, saying, Holy, holy, holy, Lord God Almighty, which was, and is, and is to come."

[57] For example, God is greater than any other conceivable being. He is perfect in his power, knowledge, wisdom, and all of his other attributes. If this were not true, then we could think of a god greater than God, but that's impossible, for our very idea of God is that of a maximally great being. So if God is perfect in all of his attributes, then he must be perfectly holy, for holiness is one of his attributes. To see this argument developed in more detail, see Morris, *Our Idea of God*, 35-56.

[58] This is not such a radical suggestion: deception is a necessary part of many other activities such as sports and acting where it isn't considered immoral by anyone. For example, a football quarterback fakes a handoff to a running back and then throws the ball to a receiver. The fake momentarily causes the defense to think that the running back has the ball, thus allowing the receiver to gain more yardage. The quarterback deceived the defense – was that immoral? I don't think so.

Beware of false prophets, which come to you in sheep's clothing, but inwardly they are ravening wolves. Ye shall know them by their fruits. Do men gather grapes of thorns, or figs of thistles? Even so every good tree bringeth forth good fruit; but a corrupt tree bringeth forth evil fruit. A good tree cannot bring forth evil fruit, neither can a corrupt tree bring forth good fruit. Every tree that bringeth not forth good fruit is hewn down, and cast into the fire. Wherefore by their fruits ye shall know them.

Jesus is saying that you can judge trees by their fruit, and via analogy, that you can judge prophets by the results of their ministries. A false prophet may look like a true prophet but the results of his preaching are bad, thus revealing that he is a false prophet. (Jesus does not elaborate exactly in what way the results are bad – perhaps they are harmfully divisive, or lead people away from God, or the predictions do not come to pass.) Although the passage has moral implications, Jesus is not making a Utilitarian analysis of what will bring about the most good (or least harm) to the greatest number of people, Nonetheless there is an example of consequentialist thinking implicit here: things are evaluated based upon their consequences, their results, their "fruit," which in ethics would be consequentialist reasoning.

What I'm arguing is that consideration of the consequences of your actions when making moral decisions is biblical. However, that does not mean that what the Bible clearly affirms is immoral becomes moral whenever it promises to bring about desirable results. Here it seems prudent to prioritize clear statements of the Bible over speculative conclusions about what the future consequences of actions are likely to be.

Another metaethical theory that was discussed is Natural Law Theory. Not for naught have Christian thinkers like Thomas Aquinas championed this approach to ethics, for the Bible provides support for the view that through rational reflection and sensitivity to the prompting of the conscience we can figure out at least the basic principles of morality. Such support is found in passages like Romans 2: 14, 15, where the Apostle Paul writes, "For when the Gentiles, which have not the law, do by nature the things contained in the law, these, having not the law, are a law unto themselves: Which shew the work of the law written in their hearts, their conscience also bearing witness..." When read in context, Paul seems to be saying that God will hold even those who do not have access to the revelation of the Hebrew Bible accountable for how they live their lives. This would seem unjust if they have no other way to know what is expected of them. Anticipating this objection, Paul states that this judgement will be on the basis of the moral knowledge that is available to them through inner reflection and the prompting of the conscience.[59]

When talking about the various forms that revelation takes, theologians make a distinction between what they term "special revelation" and what they call "general revelation." Special revelation is God's activity of communicating specific truths to specific people. Examples of this include God speaking to Moses out of the burning bush (Exodus 3), messages from God that are delivered to various people by prophets, all of the Bible, and Jesus Christ himself. General revelation, on the other hand, is the term used to describe God's activity of communicating

---

[59] It was common for first century Jews to refer to the Hebrew Bible using the merrism "the Law and the Prophets," the term "Law" referring to the earlier books of the Bible (which happen to contain much of the moral content of Hebrew Bible) and the term "Prophets" referring to the later prophetic books.

basic theological truths to all people everywhere and at all times via such media as nature (Psalm 19) and the human conscience (Romans 2:14, 15). This is called "general" both because the information revealed is of a general nature and also because it is made generally available, in other words available to everyone.

Theistic Natural Law Theory is complementary to the metaethical theory advocated in this chapter – the revelational metaethic. Theistic Natural Law Theory focuses on general revelation. The revelation metaethic advocated here has focused more on special revelation, but without excluding general revelation. In truth, the Christian metaethic needs both special and general revelation. Without a concept of general revelation it would be very difficult for the Christian ethicist to explain how those who do not consult special revelation ever succeed in discerning morality, which they clearly do.

Of course, the moral guidance provided by the Scriptures is more concrete and less ambiguous than that provided by the heart and conscience, which are currrupted by sin as is graphically described by Paul in the very next chapter of Romans.[60] Paul himself implies as much in 2:17-29 by contrasting the limited moral (and religious) knowledge that the Gentiles have with the fuller knowledge possessed by the Jews. Hence a Christian ethic should prioritize the objective moral teachings of the Bible over

---

[60] Romans 3:9-18, "What then? Are we better than they? No, in no wise: for we have before proved both Jews and Gentiles, that they are all under sin; as it is written, there is none righteous, no, not one: there is none that understandeth, there is none that seeketh after God. They are all gone out of the way, they are together become unprofitable; there is none that doeth good, no, not one. Their throat is an open sepulchre; with their tongues they have used deceit; the poison of asps is under their lips: whose mouth is full of cursing and bitterness: their feet are swift to shed blood: destruction and misery are in their ways: and the way of peace have they not known: there is no fear of God before their eyes."

127

the more subjective guidance provided by the heart and conscience.

In the end there is only one of the philosophical ethical theories that were discussed that may not have a place in a Christian ethical system: Egoism. Humans hardly need to be coached to look out for their own interests: that seems to come naturally. What we need is encouragement to *not* be egocentric. As Paul writes in Philippians 2:3, 4, "Let nothing be done through selfish ambition or conceit; but in lowliness of mind let each esteem others better than himself. Let each of you look out not only for his own interests, but for the interests of others."

Conclusion

The metaethical theory being advocated here is a **revelational Christian ethic**. Its primary source is the Bible, supported by careful thinking and sensitivity to the heart and conscience. The metaethic that we find when we read the Bible is not a simplistic "list" metaethic, but rather a sophisticated, multi-layered metaethic that involves careful interpretation and logical application and that can address any possible ethical dilemma. It incorporates the best insights of the philosophers while providing answers that philosophy does not. However, study of the Bible without the study of philosophy would fail to appreciate the metaethics implicit in the biblical passages. Therefore the conclusion follows that the best route to a satisfactory ethical system is a reasoned, intelligent study of the Bible together with philosophical ethical theory in pursuit of the goal of becoming better Christians and better people.

Questions to Ponder:

- What is the epistemological challenge of Divine Nature Theory and how can it be overcome?
- If Divine Nature Theory is true, does that mean that all of the other theories that we've discussed are false?
- Are there good reasons for believing in God?
- Are there good reasons for believing that God has revealed himself to us?
- What principles should be applied when interpreting the Bible and other difficult texts?

Terms to know:

- Hermeneutics
- Authorial intent
- Exegesis
- Eisegesis
- Grammatical-historical-contextual hermeneutic
- Deduction
- Induction
- Analogous induction
- Revelational Christian ethic
- Special revelation
- General revelation

For further reading:

- A Christian metaethic similar to that advocated in this chapter is found in Dennis P. Hollinger, *Choosing the Good: Christian Ethics in a Complex World*. Grand Rapids, MI: Baker Book House, 2002.
- Another volume that is harmonious in spirit though different in style is Arthur F. Holmes, *Ethics:*

Approaching Moral Decisions, 2nd edition. Downers Grove, IL: IVP Academic, 2007.

- A very interesting two-volume set is David K. Clark and Robert V. Rakestraw, eds. *Readings in Christian Ethics, vol. 1: Theory and Method* (Grand Rapids, MI: Baker Book House, 1994) and *vol. 2: Issues and Applications* (Grand Rapids, MI: Baker Book House, 1996). The first of these anthologies deals with issues in Christian metaethics while the second deals with Christian options and arguments in applied ethics.

Chapter Ten

Application:
The Abortion Debate

Synopsis

In this chapter we turn to applied ethics. My goal is to demonstrate how the revelational Christian metaethic described and advocated in the preceding chapters can be applied to concrete moral issues by applying it to a particular issue as an example. The issue that I have chosen is abortion. I have chosen this issue not because it is a particular hobby horse of mine, but because although it is an important issue to many people on both sides of the debate, both sides of the debate often use rather poor arguments to advance their positions.

Consistent with the metaethic that I've been advocating, I will begin with an evaluation of the biblical data that is thought to be relevant to the abortion debate. However, I will not stop there: I will also consider relevant theological and philosophical arguments. *Ultima facie* I believe that the pro-life position is the most biblically and philosophically defensible position and I will endeavor to explain why in objective terms.

Introduction

In the first chapter of this book I wrote about the importance of approaching moral dilemmas "intentionally." Many people simply absorb their moral beliefs from the culture around them – very little conscious choice is involved. However, this approach to morality is not likely to result in a coherent set of moral beliefs. It is also likely to result in some beliefs that are simply not true. That is why I suggested that it would be better for us to be "intentional" about morality: to approach morality thoughtfully and rationally so as to devise a reliable methodology for determining what is right and wrong (metaethics) and then systematically apply this methodology to the various dilemmas that we are likely to face (applied ethics).

We have now accomplished the first part of this project: we have examined a wide range of ethical methodologies and devised an approach that we believe is most likely to result in sound ethical decisions. I've called this approach a revelational Christian ethic, for it has as its center the revelation of the perfectly holy God who is the source of morality. Now I want to provide an example of applying this metaethic to an issue in applied ethics. The issue that I have selected is abortion, which has been an enormous source of moral controversy for the last fifty years.

Theory

The institution where I teach is well known for having a pro-life ethos on campus. Hence I've heard many speakers and read many articles defending the pro-life position. Along the way I've seen and heard many arguments in support of this position. Many of these arguments have been, in my professional opinion, very weak. Regardless of how right your position is – or how right you *think* it is – it cannot be shown to be right by using bad arguments. If the truth really is on your side, then you should be able to come up with good arguments showing that it is. If the pro-life position is right, then pro-life advocates should be able to come up with sound arguments in its defense.

On the other hand, over the years I've seen many weak arguments for the pro-choice position, too. And what is bad for the goose is bad for the gander, as they don't say but surely could. What I mean by a "weak argument" is an argument that, if examined objectively, would not succeed in showing that the conclusion is probably true. Several factors can render an argument weak in this sense, including dubious presuppositions, inaccurate data, and faulty logic. When discussing important issues like abortion, a person's strong feelings on the issue may blind him to his own presuppositions, flaws in the data, and invalid logic. Hence the value of objectivity.

Objectivity, however, is not always as easy to achieve as you might think. We naturally see the logic of our own position and struggle to see the logic of any position that is in tension with our own. Furthermore, we are often more aware of data that supports our position then we are of data that contravenes it, even if a significant body of contrary data exists. This being the case, it is easy to see why two people can have very strong convictions toward opposite positions on abortion. And these strong convictions and their aforementioned causes make it hard for them to dispassionately and objectively consider the opposing side.

One thing that would help increase our objectivity when considering the question of abortion is reading more broadly in the literature supporting the other side. This means that pro-life advocates need to read articles defending the pro-choice position and pro-choice advocates need to read articles defending the pro-life position. The result of this, were it to happen, would be a greater awareness on both sides of the data and arguments that support the other position. It would also bring both sides into contact with counters to their own arguments, which would help them to understand why the other side does not find these arguments as convincing as the first side does.

I know that some who have very strong convictions on both sides of the abortion debate will react to this suggestion with distaste, feeling like it would be traitorous to read widely the literature of the opposing camp. But unless we are willing to say that we can know that our position is right even though we have not looked at the

evidence and argumentation supporting the other side –
which seems to be an egregious example of jumping to a
conclusion – we need to look at both sides before we can
draw an informed conclusion on the matter. In other words,
if truth is our goal, we shouldn't be afraid to look
objectively at arguments that oppose our position, even in
the abortion debate.

Unfortunately, I've known people on both sides
who are not willing to look objectively at the arguments for
the opposing view. This suggests to me that some people in
this debate are more devoted to their position than to truth
itself. That's dangerous, and it's epistemically
irresponsible, too.

Christians who truly want to defend the moral
position must undertake an objective analysis of arguments
for and against each side in the debate. We must approach
the issue as Christians, but we must not assume that the
Christian position is automatically pro-life or pro-choice,
for that would compromise our objectivity, and besides,
there have long been Christians on both sides of this
issue.[61]

What interests me in this chapter is the question of
whether or not Christians should view abortion as moral.
I'm not going to explore whether abortion should be legal
or illegal, and this is an important point that I ask you to
keep in mind. Not all things that are immoral are also
illegal, and not all things that are illegal are inherently

---

[61] A short and popular article on the evolution of the Evangelical
attitude toward abortion is Fred Clark's "The 'biblical view' that's
younger than the Happy Meal," *Patheos*, February 18, 2012,
http://www.patheos.com/blogs/slacktivist/2012/02/18/the-biblical-
view-thats-younger-than-the-happy-meal/ (accessed March 12, 2016).
A scientific study of attitude change across American religious
traditions is John P. Hoffmann and Sherrie Mills Johnson, "Attitudes
toward Abortion among Religious Traditions in the United States:
Change or Continuity?" *Sociology of Religion* 66: 2, 161-182.

immoral aside from being prohibited by the law. The question of the relationship of morality to legislation is very interesting but would require a complete chapter unto itself. Nor will I discuss how Christians should respond to abortion advocates in the public debate over the issue or other such related topics. I am strictly limiting my discussion to the morality of the issue.

In keeping with the revelational metaethic advocated in the preceding chapter, I would like to begin with an examination of what God has revealed on this issue. So let us turn to an examination of what the Bible says that is relevant to abortion. First we will look at some attempts to use the Bible to throw light on this issue that I think do not work. Then we'll proceed to stronger arguments.

Relevant Bible Passages

Many Christians seem to think that the Bible is clearly on the pro-life side in this debate. There are, however, pro-choice Christians who use the Bible in support of their position. The biblical passage that I've most often seen used in support of the position that a fetus is not a person and therefore aborting it is not immoral is Genesis 2:7, "And the LORD God formed man of the dust of the ground, and breathed into his nostrils the breath of life; and man became a living soul." The context in which this verse occurs is predominantly historical: most of Genesis reads as a historical account of the earliest stages of development of the nation of Israel. The first several chapters can be read either as a literal account or an allegorical account of the creation of the world. Whether these chapters, which include the verse in question, are taken literally or as an allegory is not important for our purposes, so I will not opine about which of these approaches to the early chapters seems most justified. Regardless of whether this is a literal or allegorical account of the creation of the first human, it seems to portray Adam's life as not beginning until breath enters his lungs.

Pro-life Christians typically argue that the Bible supports the view that human life begins long before a baby takes its first breath. However, that does not appear to be the case with Adam, whose life appears to have begun simultaneously with his first breath. However, inferring from this that, for all humans subsequent to Adam, life also begins with the first breath would commit the fallacy of **forgetful induction**. This fallacy involves considering only the evidence that supports your conclusion and ignoring (or conveniently "forgetting") evidence that undermines your conclusion. In the case of Adam, those who take the beginning of his life as paradigmatic for the beginning of all life are forgetting the many significant differences between Adam and subsequent humans that are pertinent to the question of when life begins for those humans.[62] Therefore the argument from Genesis 2:7 does not seem very strong.

Another passage that is used by Pro-choice Christians is Exodus 21:22-25, which says:

> If men strive, and hurt a woman with child, so that her fruit depart from her, and yet no mischief follow: he shall be surely punished, according as the

---

[62] For one thing, Adam (and Eve) did not have the same kind of conception/development/birth process that subsequent humans have had. Furthermore, if you hold that personhood is somehow contingent on having breath, then you face the problem of having to affirm that those who cannot breathe are not persons. This is a problem because there are clear counterexamples to it: one who is receiving oxygenated blood during lung replacement surgery continues to be a person, and it seems medically possible that a fetus could be born and grow up being dependent on something like oxygenated blood for her whole life, but such an individual would still be a person.

woman's husband will lay upon him; and he shall pay as the judges determine. And if any mischief follow, then thou shalt give life for life, eye for eye, tooth for tooth, hand for hand, foot for foot, burning for burning, wound for wound, stripe for stripe.

Interestingly, pro-life advocates sometimes use this same passage in support of their position. They interpret this passage as saying that if a man causes a women to give birth prematurely but there is no harm to the infant, then the offending man will pay a lesser penalty than if the injury results in harm to the infant. But if the offense results in the death of the child, the penalty that the man must pay is his own life. This imposition of the death penalty is taken as an indication that the life of the fetus is valued in the same manner as the life of an adult.

However, pro-choice commentators point out problems with this interpretation. The pro-life interpretation depends on construing the phrase "if any mischief follow" as referring to ill effects suffered by the fetus or infant. However, the penalties imposed seem to be a better fit with injuries to the mother: the fetus or infant would not have teeth to lose, so "tooth for tooth" seems particularly problematic to the pro-life interpretation, but the likelihood of damage to the eye, hand, foot, or skin of the pre-natal infant as a result of such an altercation also seems less than the likelihood that the mother would suffer such injuries. So it could be that the death penalty recommended here is punishment for injury resulting in the death of the mother rather than death of the fetus or infant.

The pro-choice reading of this passage interprets it as imposing a smaller penalty at first because there is less harm to the women and a larger penalty only if there is more significant harm to the women, like the loss of a tooth or an eye, and the death penalty if she loses her life. This seems like a reasonable interpretation of the passage.

However, this passage occurs very early in the Hebrew Bible and is not necessarily the Bible's final word on the issue. There is contextual evidence that the moral precepts taught in this passage are provisional rather than normative for all times.

Here we must keep in mind the concept of **progressive revelation**: early in the Bible God reveals basic truths in a simple way, accommodating the communication of his message to the level and abilities of his audience. As time passes God adds to the message, gradually revealing more and more truth. By the time of the New Testament a much higher level of moral and spiritual understanding has been attained.[63] The chapter in which this passage occurs (Exodus 21) is very early in the Bible, and therefore represents an early stage in God's revelational program. It contains other moral teachings that clearly do not represent the fullness of morality found in later portions of the Bible. For example, while the punishment for negligence resulting in a man's bull causing the death of someone else's wife or child is the death of the bull and of the bull's owner, if the deceased is the man's servant, the penalty is merely the death of the bull and a fine of 30 shekels of silver. It seems that the life of a servant is not valued as highly as the life of a free woman or child. By the time of the New Testament, however, a more egalitarian valuation of human worth seems to be in place.

Similarly, it could be the case that Exodus 21 accurately reflects a low valuation of the life of a fetus prior to exiting the womb, but it could also be the case that this is not the final word on the value of fetal life according to the Bible. The question, then, is what the rest of the

---

[63] The concept of progressive revelation seems to be implied by Jesus in Matthew 19:1-9.

Bible says on this issue. Are there other, perhaps later passages that speak unambiguously on this topic?

Many pro-life Christians believe that Jeremiah 1:4, 5 unambiguously supports their position. It says, "Then the word of the LORD came unto me, saying, Before I formed thee in the belly I knew thee; and before thou camest forth out of the womb I sanctified thee, and I ordained thee a prophet unto the nations." Some think that because God knew Jeremiah before he was born, Jeremiah must have been a person (in the sense relevant to the abortion debate) prior to his actual birth. This seems to them to entail that not only the fetus but even the zygote is a person.[64] And because taking the life of an innocent person (if a zygote is a person, it is about as innocent as any person can be) is murder, they conclude that abortion is murder.

But of course if this interpretation of these verses is correct, then it would imply that Jeremiah was a person (in the relevant sense) even prior to conception, since God, who is omniscient, knew Jeremiah from eternity past. If that's the case, then the personhood of Jeremiah would seem to be independent of his physical body, which leads to difficult questions about the relationship of the death of the body to the death of the person and perhaps fatally undermines the use of this passage in the pro-life cause. This is because the pro-life position is usually predicated on the conviction that abortion ends not merely the life of a collection of tissues but the life of a person. However, if Jeremiah was a person before having a body, then it seems possible that he remains a person after the demise of his body, too. If this is correct, then abortion would end the life of the body but not the life of the person. But then what is the difference between the pro-choice belief that abortion kills only a collection of tissues and this version of the pro-

---

[64] A **zygote** is the fertilized egg prior to dividing to form the embryo. An **embryo** is the developing baby up to about two months, when the features become recognizably human. After that it is called a **fetus**.

life position, which holds that abortion kills the body but does not kill the actual person?[65]

A similar passage is Psalm 139:13ff, which is often used to show that human life begins at conception and that therefore abortion is murder. Verses 13-15 say,

> ...thou hast possessed my reins: thou hast covered me in my mother's womb. I will praise thee; for I am fearfully and wonderfully made: marvellous are thy works; and that my soul knoweth right well. My substance was not hid from thee, when I was made in secret, and curiously wrought in the lowest parts of the earth.

This passage is sometimes taken to imply both that God knew the psalmist before his birth and that what is developing in the womb is identified with the psalmist, thus showing that the zygote or embryo or fetus is a person. That God knew the psalmist before his birth is neither particularly controversial (for Christians) nor relevant to the debate. The second point, though, may be, and therefore it requires a little more reflection.

In identifying himself with the fetus, is the psalmist saying that the fetus is a person in the sense relevant to the abortion debate? Perhaps, but it's not completely clear. For one thing, this is poetry, not didactic writing, and thus we ought to be cautious about reading too much into the details of these descriptions. Furthermore, that the psalmist identifies with the fetus does not entail that the fetus is the psalmist in the full sense needed for the abortion debate. I could say something like, "Back when they were building

---

[65] A potential response to this is that the body belongs to the person, and killing it is killing the body of another person, which is just as wrong when done to a fetus as when done to an adult. This position carries with it considerable metaphysical baggage, but it is baggage that some would not object to bearing.

my house, they failed to pour a good foundation for it." In this case I would be identifying the very beginnings of my house with the completed house in which I now live, but the house as it existed then would have neither the form nor the function of a house. It was not a house, even though by the rules of the English language I can now refer to it as "my house." Likewise it's possible for the psalmist to refer to what was being formed in his mother's womb as himself, even if at the time it wasn't yet him. Careful thought is required here, and we must resist the temptation to read what is useful to our cause back into passages like this.

Relevant Theological Considerations

In addition to biblical arguments Christians also employ theological arguments in support of their preferred positions in the abortion debate. One such argument is the following:

> The most problematic of them all for those who claim authority for the Biblical text yet support abortion are the accounts surrounding the conception and birth of Jesus Christ. There are enormous Christological problems that arise if one assumes that the pre-born are not persons, not truly human. If none of us are persons before birth, then that means that, for nine months, the being contained in the Virgin's womb is fully God and fully something else, but not human. Fully what? I'd really like to know. What exactly did the divine Son of God take to Himself for those nine months? He wasn't the God-man, but the God-fetus? What

kind of pre-born Christological hybrid horror is that in there, anyway?[66]

Now we certainly can agree that Christian orthodoxy affirms both the full deity and the full humanity of Jesus Christ. However, this does not entail that it affirms that for all of the life of the human Jesus he was a human *person* in the sense relevant to the abortion debate. There is an important distinction between being a human and being a person to which we will return shortly. For now I'll simply point out that not all human flesh is a human person. As I write this I am watching two members of the Liberty University Fencing Club dueling with sabers. Should one lop off the finger of the other, that finger would continue to be human flesh, but it would not be a human person.

The passage cited is arguing that if a fetus is human then it is a person. It **conflates** the concepts of humanness and personhood in a way that is problematic. This is especially evident when the author writes, "There are enormous Christological problems that arise if one assumes that the pre-born are not persons, not truly human." But I think that the pro-choice response to this is correct: as already noted, something can be human without being a person.[67]

---

[66] Andrew Stephen Damick, "The 'Biblical' Argument for Abortion," *Orthodoxy and Heterodoxy*, July 31, 2012 http://orthodoxyandheterodoxy.org/2012/07/31/the-biblical-argument-for-abortion/ (accessed March 12, 2016).

[67] **Conflation** is blending two things together to make one new one, such as blending two storylines to make a new story that is a hybrid of the two old originals. This is not always bad, obviously, but it is a fallacy when it is done in an argument like this because it hides important differences between two things that would undermine the argument were they brought to light. In the passage cited the author makes it seem that denial of the personhood of the fetus is also a denial of the humanity of the fetus, but that's clearly not the case.

To make matters even worse, the passage also seems to commit the fallacy of **equivocation**. To equivocate is to use a term in two different ways in an argument while making it look like you're using it in the same way throughout. Here the first time the word "human" is used it's clearly intended as a synonym for "person": "...if one assumes that the pre-born are not persons, not truly human." But the second time the term is used the author seems to be implying that the pro-choice view results in the conclusion that the prenatal Jesus belonged to something other than the human race, as if they hold that he was a Martian or some sort of monstrosity. Notice the attempted *reductio ad absurdum* that depends on Jesus being viewed as outside of the human race: "...the being contained in the Virgin's womb is fully God and fully something else, but not human. What kind of pre-born Christological hybrid horror is that in there, anyway?" This is clearly a **straw man**, for pro-choice advocates neither hold that a human fetus is not human nor that it is a monstrosity.[68]

Another theological argument that is obviously relevant to the abortion debate is the doctrine that humans bear the image of God (*imago dei*). In fact, this is perhaps the root of the prohibition of murder, for Genesis 9:6 states, "Whoso sheddeth man's blood, by man shall his blood be shed: for in the image of God made he man." There appears to be some sense in which ending a life dishonors God himself, defacing his image reflected by the living human person. Hence if a fetus is a living human person who

---

[68] The straw man fallacy involves portraying a position in a way that makes it unfairly vulnerable to attack. Just as a real person could easily defeat a scarecrow in a fight but doing so would not prove anything about that person's fighting ability, so too a debater can easily repudiate a position if it is a straw man, but doing so would not show that the underlying position is wrong or that his or her own view is correct.

reflects God's image, to end its life would be as immoral as is ending the life of a human adult. We cannot simply assume, though, that a fetus is a living human person. At least we cannot do so without begging the question.[69] And whether a fetus is a living human person is a rather philosophical question. So let's turn our attention to philosophical arguments against abortion.

Philosophical Arguments

Many pro-life advocates make one particular type of philosophical mistake when arguing for their position. It occurs in at least three forms. The first of these is to think that they gain something in this debate by showing that a fetus is alive. Since no pro-choice advocates are arguing that a fetus isn't alive, this argument doesn't accomplish anything useful to the pro-life cause. Pro-choice advocates recognize that the fetus is alive. They do not recognize that causing it to cease being alive is a problem. To them doing so seems no more problematic than removing an unwanted growth would be. Sometimes the pro-life position shifts the vocabulary of this discussion a little, arguing that the fetus is "a life," which has the potential to be a better way of arguing, but sometimes I get the impression that they don't mean anything more by this than that it is alive.

The second form that I see this mistake take is the form of an argument about the humanity of the fetus. Pro-life advocates frequently make a big point of showing that the fetus is human, often proffering an array of medical data that strongly supports this conclusion. Again, since the pro-choice side is not arguing that the fetus is anything

---

[69] As explained much earlier, to "beg the question" is to assume in your argument the truth of the very issue that is being debated. Begging the question is a fallacious form of reasoning.

other than human, this is of dubious value. The pro-choice side is not arguing that it's chimpanzee, gorilla, orangutan, Neanderthal, Cro-Magnon, or alien. It accepts that the fetus is human as well as that it's alive, though of course an unwanted growth like cancer or a wart can also be human and alive.

Third, pro-life advocates sometimes argue that the fetus is genetically distinct from its mother. This is perhaps a helpful point, for it shows that the fetus is not just a part of the mother, like tonsils or a mole are. However, it falls short of being a sufficient condition for the pro-life position, for showing that the fetus is not the mother does not show that the fetus is someone else.[70]

One might think that combining these three points in order to demonstrate that the fetus is a distinct human life would be sufficient for the pro-life position, at least for those who accept that it is wrong to take human life. I think it comes close, but it is still not sufficient. Imagine a scenario in which a person who has signed up as an organ donor passes away. Let's call her Renee. Her organs are harvested, including the pineal gland in her brain. As we all know, some people[71] have thought that this gland is the critical link between the body and the mind, in which case having a healthy pineal gland would be very important to one's mental state. But then the organ bank learns that there are no surgeons who perform pineal-gland-replacement surgery, so they make the decision to no longer sustain the donated but unneeded gland. This gland, while it was yet living, was alive, human, and genetically distinct. But would anyone argue that taking it off of life support is murder? I doubt it.

---

[70] My point here is that showing that the fetus is *something* else does not show that it is *someone* else (that it is another person). I'll briefly discuss the issue of personhood soon.

[71] Most notably Descartes, of course.

146

Why isn't terminating the life of the pineal gland murder? It is terminating life. For that matter, it's terminating human life. But it's not terminating the life of *a person*, and I think that's the crucial issue that has been missing from the previous arguments: personhood.

It seems to me that the root disagreement between thoughtful pro-lifers and reflective pro-choicers is over the personhood of the fetus.[72] The pro-life side believes that a fetus is a small person (some say that it "has the potential to be or become a person"), while the pro-choice side believes that the fetus is not a person. And perhaps there's a connection between personhood and the *imago dei*. Perhaps it is, at least in part, the fact that we are *persons* that causes us to reflect God's nature, for God too is a person.

If I'm right about the central importance of personhood in this debate, then the relevant question to be answered is, "When does personhood begin?" This is a difficult question, though. To answer it, we may need to answer another difficult question: what is personhood? These questions may not be impossible to answer, but they require a degree of metaphysical and logical technicality that goes far beyond the scope of this book. Therefore I'm going to approach the question of the beginning of personhood biblically rather than philosophically.

---

[72] Judith Jarvis Thomson is a notable exception to this. In her acclaimed 1971 article "A Defense of Abortion" she grants for the sake of argument that the fetus is a person yet still argues for abortion in many circumstances. Judith Jarvis Thomson, "A Defense of Abortion," *Philosophy & Public Affairs* 1:1 (Autumn 1971), 47-66. There have been several cogent responses to Thomson; see for example David Boonin-Vail, "Death Comes for the Violinist: On Two Objections to Thomson's 'Defense of Abortion,'" *Social Theory and Practice* 23.3 (Fall 1997): 329-64. In subsequent publications Thomson has defended and updated her arguments.

A Stronger Biblical Pro-life Argument

I believe that there are biblical arguments available to the pro-life cause that are stronger than those previously repudiated in this chapter. One comes from the scriptural description of John the Baptist, who is said to have been "filled with the Holy Spirit, even from his mother's womb" (Luke 1:15).[73] No biblical passage mentions a non-person being filled with the Holy Spirit in this sense. All references to the filling of the Holy Spirit concern the filling of a person. If it is the case that the Holy Spirit only

---

[73] There is some discussion among Bible scholars about whether the phrase "from his mother's womb" is simply a poetic way of saying "from birth" or whether it includes the time that the developing child spends in the womb prior to birth. The phrase (in various permutations) occurs a number of times in the Bible. Only one provides data that is clearly relevant to this question: Judges 13:4, 5, "Now therefore beware, I pray thee, and drink not wine nor strong drink, and eat not any unclean thing: For, lo, thou shalt conceive, and bear a son; and no razor shall come on his head: for the child shall be a Nazarite unto God from the womb: and he shall begin to deliver Israel out of the hand of the Philistines." Here we see that if Samson's mother had eaten anything unclean while Samson was still in the womb it would have violated his status as a Nazarite just as if he himself had eaten something unclean after being born. In this passage the phrase "from the womb" includes the time when Samson was in the womb. This sheds light on the Lukan phrase "from his mother's womb" because in Judges 16:17 Samson uses the language found in Luke (there are linguistic differences, of course: Samson was speaking Hebrew while Luke was writing Greek) to indicate the beginning of his time as a Nazarite, "...he told her all his heart, and said unto her. There hath not come a razor upon mine head; for I have been a Nazarite unto God from my mother's womb: if I be shaven, then my strength will go from me, and I shall become weak, and be like any other man." Since his time as a Nazarite includes his time in the womb, we can safely conclude that Samson understands the phrase "my mother's womb" to include the time in the womb. Lacking strong arguments to the contrary, it seems likely that Luke is using the phrase in a similar way. A similar argument for personhood beginning in the womb could be constructed using these passages in Judges.

fills persons, then this passage indicates that John-the-fetal-Baptist was a person even when he was in Elizabeth's womb. And although John certainly was an exceptional figure, I think we can affirm that he was also a normal human being who is sufficiently analogous to other humans that we can use his prenatal personhood to conclude that if he was a person while he was an embryo, then other embryos are, at least in general, persons, too.[74]

A second argument comes from John-the-fetal-Baptist's response to the voice of Mary the mother of Jesus. This is described by Elizabeth as jumping for joy in the womb (see Luke 1:41&44). While the capacity to feel emotions probably does not entail the existence of consciousness, self-awareness, or some of the other qualities that are sometimes thought to be indicators of personhood, the ability to have emotions and to respond emotionally to stimuli seems to indicate a higher degree of sentience than mere tissue would have. This provides evidence that we are dealing with more than merely a collection of human tissues.

Because of biblical considerations like these I am strongly inclined to grant personhood to fetuses. And since the same arguments support granting personhood to embryos and zygotes, I am strongly inclined to view them as persons, too.[75] Even though my arguments for the personhood of zygotes and embryos do not form an air-tight case, it seems preferable to err on the side of caution and not take a zygote's life rather than to err on the side of abortion since there is at least a reasonable possibility that zygotes and embryos are persons. We could say that we

---

[74] The logic of this argument is analogous induction. Deceased embryos would most likely be an exception to the rule: they are most likely not persons.

[75] The argument from the fetal John the Baptist jumping in Elizabeth's womb may only apply to fetuses, since Luke 1:36 indicates that this happened during the sixth month of Elizabeth's pregnancy.

should at the very least give them "the benefit of the doubt." Therefore I find myself in the pro-life camp.

A Common Ground Argument against Abortion

How I've argued to this conclusion is, I admit, in a specific way rather problematic. If Christians conclude that a zygote is a human life that should be protected, but they conclude this by using uniquely Christian sources that are not accepted by the rest of society, how can Christians hope to protect fetal life? We must find **common ground arguments** in order to accomplish this mission.[76] We've often failed to do this, perhaps because we don't clearly see why we should, but indeed we must. Can it be done? I think so. Showing that personhood begins at conception is a difficult task, but perhaps it's not a prerequisite to the argument that fetal life should be protected.

　　Strategically, it may be useful to get both sides to recognize the difficulty of this question. The question of when *life* begins is not really relevant – life is there even before conception. The question of whether fetal life is *human* is not difficult – the DNA makes that incontrovertible. The difficult question is, when does a new, independent human *person* begin? What is the beginning of personhood? Sometimes the position that it begins at conception seems to be just as arbitrary as the

---

[76] Common ground arguments are arguments that anyone, or at least nearly anyone, in a society could find reasonable. Finding and appealing to common ground greatly facilitates conflict resolution. Arguments that appeal to the Bible are not common ground arguments because those who do not believe that the Bible is the word of God will not find them persuasive. On the other hand, arguments that attempt to show that some course of action will be beneficial to all of society are a good example of common ground arguments.

The Sorites Paradox and Abortion

Eubulides of Miletus was a contemporary of Aristotle who specialized in paradoxes. One of his paradoxes is named the Sorites Paradox after the Greek word for a pile or heap (σοριτες). The paradox arises when we realize that adding one grain of sand to another doesn't make a heap, nor will adding another, yet if we continue to add grains we eventually will have a heap. But when exactly do these grains become a heap – after the 100th grain, or the 500th, or the 5000th? Anywhere we draw the line seems to be arbitrary. The question of when an ovum becomes a person may be like this – there may not be a clear answer. Is it when the sperm first penetrates the cell wall, or when the zygote divides and forms an embryo, or when the embryo divides the first time, making four cells, or the second time, so there are eight cells…we could go on and on, but unless we have some principled reason to draw the line where we do, our line-drawing will simply be arbitrary.

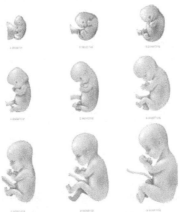

position that it begins at birth. Another position is that it begins once the central nervous system is developed. Some opt for this because it seems to them that this is when consciousness becomes a theoretical possibility. However, if consciousness is necessary to personhood, then those who are unconscious are not persons, which seems like an unlikely conclusion. Knock someone out before you kill him and it's no longer murder? Highly implausible.

Of course, there are those who argue that, in light of the uncertainty of the personhood of an embryo or a fetus, the burden on a single parent of raising a child is so great that it justifies ending the embryo's life through an abortion. This same reasoning has been used by some ethicists to argue for post-natal abortion, too.[77] This raises the specter of someone arguing that in any situation where the burden of one person on another is sufficient, the latter is justified in terminating the former. This could apply to unwanted children, troublesome teenagers, adults who never leave home, even senior parents who cannot take care of themselves. This seems like a path to be avoided.[78]

---

[77] Perhaps most notably Peter Singer, see for example ch. 6, "Taking Life: Humans," *Practical Ethics* 2nd edition (Cambridge: Cambridge University Press, 1993).

[78] Here we must be careful not to commit the **slippery slope fallacy**. This fallacy occurs when you assume or assert that some consequence or consequences will follow from a certain action without providing adequate justification for that assumption. For example, some people vocally assert that allowing any kind of firearm regulation will eventually lead to a total ban on private ownership of firearms in the US. This is an example of the slippery slope fallacy if the person making the assertion does not have sufficient evidence to back up the assertion. In this example it would be safer for the person to say that he or she is concerned that it *might* lead to such a ban, but even that assertion should be accompanied by supporting evidence. My argument about the burden on a single parent does not involve a slippery slope because 1. It is supported by the evidence that the application of the standard of "too great a burden" has already been broadened beyond pre-natal abortion, and 2. The logic of my argument is not that one

In light of the difficulty of determining the beginning of personhood, perhaps the morally responsible position would be to: 1. Admit that we don't know, and 2. Therefore be very cautious about ending the life of anything that could reasonably be thought to be a candidate for personhood. My proposal is that the most prudent position is also the most careful one: we should avoid ending human life from the earliest point where it might even possibly constitute personhood. This would be, I believe, conception. **Absent some compelling reason to think that personhood cannot have its beginning at conception, protecting all life after conception seems sensible.** So we must ask if there is any compelling reason to think that life could not begin at conception. Several such arguments have been advanced, so let's consider them.

Conception is a process, not a distinct point in time.

It has been argued that conception, or fertilization, is a series or process that occurs over time. It is not quite like throwing a switch: it's more like adding apples until you go from having no apples to having a full bushel. We begin with a sperm and an ovum, the sperm penetrates the ovum, the sperm forms a separate nucleus within the ovum, the sperm nucleus and the ovum nucleus merge, etc. At which point does "conception" occur? It's a rather arbitrary line in the sand, a term or concept that we have created to represent an idea as if it is a moment in time when in fact

---

thing will lead to another but rather that there is a strong analogy between abortion and unwanted children, etc., when it comes to the burden that they represent to those who responsible for them.

the idea represents a series of steps and the resulting situation.

All of this is true, but it does not in any way lessen the importance of the issue at hand. It simply forces us to refine our inquiry. The most salient question is, "At what point are we morally obligated to avoid aborting the ovum in the process of becoming a zygote?" Consistent with what I am advocating, I think the most reasonable answer is that we should avoid aborting the ovum at the earliest point that it could possibly be a zygote, which is when the sperm first penetrates the ovum. This objection does not overthrow my position, it simply forces me to clarify the details.

Twins and clones

Another objection to zygote personhood arises from the process through which identical twins are formed. If personhood begins as early as the fertilized ovum, or even as early as the zygote, this gives rise to some difficult questions about the nature of a human person. If a zygote is a person, then that zygote has a soul according to the Christian tradition. But in the case of identical twins, the zygote divides to form two persons. Does the soul divide? Can an immaterial substance "divide"?[79]

A similar problem arises related to cloning. If a human were to be cloned, would her clone not be a person, since she was never "conceived" – she was never a fertilized ovum? Would she have a soul at all?[80]

---

[79] The probable conclusion that immaterial substances cannot divide may be a clue that this whole question is misguided. Perhaps both halves of the embryo are ensouled without any division of the soul being necessary.

[80] While conception may be one way for a human person to begin and for a zygote to be ensouled, that does not mean that it is the only way.

These objections are intended to cast doubt on the personhood of the zygote. And perhaps they do (though I am not convinced), but they do not rule it out. Consistent with my cautious approach, I would say that we should treat twin zygotes and cloned zygotes as if they are persons even if we are not certain that they are.

Failure of an embryo to implant and other natural abortions

Medical experts tell us that only a fraction of zygotes actually successfully implant in the womb. The great majority of zygotes fail to implant and are naturally aborted. If zygotes are persons, we should probably mourn their passing, but we don't.

This is a *reductio ad absurdum* argument against the view that zygotes are persons. But perhaps we *should* mourn such deaths – except that we are rarely aware when they occur. However, I personally know several women who have suffered miscarriages and have mourned the loss of their "baby." I don't think this argument disproves the personhood of zygotes, nor does it overthrow my cautious approach to preserving human life.

Conclusion

Lacking a strong argument *against* the personhood of zygotes, and without needing a strong argument *for* the personhood of zygotes, I think we can confidently say that the life of zygotes should be protected. I recognize, of

---

It seems at least theoretically possible that cloning would also result in an ensouled human person.

course, that there are influential pro-choice arguments that I have not addressed. For example, I have not discussed the category of arguments that contend that abortion is moral in specific circumstances such as when the pregnancy is the result of rape, when the fetus has significant medical impairments, or when the pregnancy threatens the life of the mother. Undoubtedly these are important considerations that require our attention. And although I am not going to address them at this time, I believe that my approach lays a foundation for adequately dealing with them in a way that respects the life of the zygote/embryo/fetus. With this cautious life-affirming approach we can respond objectively to a wide range of arguments without denying their cogency but at the same time prioritizing the value of life.

Questions to Ponder:

- What is the difference between an act being illegal and an act being immoral?
- Is it a good idea to legislate morality?
- If one person has a strong conviction that something is immoral and another person has an equally strong conviction that it is moral, should either be able to force the other to live contrary to his or her own convictions?
- If someone who is pro-choice reads this chapter, he or she will be faced with a decision: either concede my arguments and change positions or show how my arguments fail. Can you think of cogent pro-choice counters to my pro-life arguments?

Terms to know:
Forgetful induction
Progressive revelation
Ovum
Zygote
Embryo
Fetus
Conflation
Equivocation
Straw man
Common ground argument
Slippery slope fallacy

For further reading:
- Some helpful quick-reference resources for Christian ethics are:
    - *Dictionary of Scripture and Ethics*, Joel B. Green, ed. Grand Rapids: Baker Academic, 2012.
    - Stanley J. Grenz and Jay T. Smith, *Pocket Dictionary of Ethics: Over 300 Terms & Ideas Clearly & Concisely Defined*. Downers Grove, IL: IVP Pocket Reference, 2003.
- A nice anthology on applied ethics is Owen Smith and Anne Smith, eds., *Taking Sides: Clashing Views on Moral Issues* 14th edition. New York: McGraw-Hill Education, 2014. This book covers a range of issues in applied ethics, presenting arguments for opposing sides on each issue written by people who are strongly convinced that their approach is the most moral one. If you want to understand both sides of an issue, this is a good place to begin.
- Another helpful anthology is Theodore C. Denise, Nicholas White, and Sheldon P. Peterfreund, eds.,

Great Traditions in Ethics 12th edition. Boston: Wadsworth, 2007. This collection of primary texts helps the reader to see how ethical thought has developed from ancient times to today, giving the reader insight into why we view things the way that we do.

Afterword

Closing Thoughts for the Reader

The goal of this book has been to enable you, the reader, to rationally and systematically evaluate moral beliefs so that you can know whether your own moral beliefs are justified, and if they are, how they are. Being able to do this is important, for it enables you to know that your convictions are not merely unfounded opinion. Furthermore, it prepares you to approach future moral dilemmas in a way that will maximize your ability to arrive at the best conclusions.

I've done this by familiarizing you with some basic principles of logical reasoning, by introducing to you a range of strategies that people have developed to determine what is moral, by critically examining these strategies to discover their strengths and weaknesses, and ultimately by arguing for a metaethic that sees God's nature as determinative of morality and God's revelation as key to discovering it. The various philosophical metaethical theories previously examined were seen to be complementary to the revelational Christian metaethic that I advocate.

The book finished with an application of the revelational Christian metaethic to a very controversial and divisive issue in contemporary ethics: abortion. This metaethic can be applied in a similar fashion to a great many other issues – in fact, I believe that it can be applied to every issue in applied ethics. I make no attempt to do so here, but I am confident that the reader who has followed the argument of the book closely has made a solid start down the path toward mastering the skills necessary to apply this metaethic on his or her own.

For the reader who has enjoyed this introduction to ethical theory and would like to read more, I remind you of the recommended readings at the end of each of the book's chapters. They are there specifically for you! May God bless you as you continue to grow in your knowledge of the moral truths that he has revealed to us.

Sincerely,

Michael S. Jones

Index

CPSIA information can be obtained
at www.ICGtesting.com
Printed in the USA
LVHW012247131118
596878LV00001B/1/P